Melvin Gorham's Interpretation

of

Richard Wagner's

THE RHINEGOLD

Illustrations by Sanguine

Published by
SOVEREIGN PRESS
326 Harris Road
Rochester, WA 98579

ISBN 0-914752-28-6

Library of Congress Catalog Card Number 89−92364

Manufactured in the United States of America

Feeling the power that they represent, as if they, themselves, were
the phantom giants sitting at the table, the representatives of
FASOLT and FAFNER look over the maps and contracts. Chapter V

BACKGROUND

Scene: The world.
Time: After the atomic wars.
Narrator: A young survivor.

Since the atomic wars of the last two generations there are very few such scholars as I who are able to read and write, but the story I have to tell merits all the permanence it can be given. Many mistakes might be avoided if things now known could be passed on to new generations. However it is already difficult to describe things that no longer exist, and that difficulty will increase as language and thought patterns continue to change. An accurate record in language now understood may be of help even though it may become a puzzle.

I would like to "date" these events. That is not easy. There appears to have been many systems for telling when things happened in relation to chosen points in time. Our concept of a year, as the time required for the earth to circle the sun, appears to have been in common use when these things took place, but datum points on which dating systems were built were radically different.

What is called the Chinese system says that man's past is a series of alternating cycles consisting of eras of dragon rule followed by eras of heaven rule, and these repeat continuously. According to that system, these happenings took place at a change from an era of dragon rule to an era of heaven rule.

Dragon rule seems to refer to an era of belief in, and respect for, fictitious group-entities. Depending on who is telling the story, these are given such names as dragons, nations, giants, bodies politic, states, and numerous others.

Heaven rule appears to refer to an era when people live as individuals freely under the open sky.

The individual people who lived through the last era of dragon rule and still retained their individual integrity called themselves "sovereigns" to distinguish themselves from those they called "brainwashed zombis" — those who never recovered from the conditioning, or "education," to which they were subjected during the dragon rule. This conditioning had made them think and act as if they were cell-like components, or "citizens," of the fictitious entities.

5

There seems to be no real conflict between what is called the Chinese system of dating events and that which orients on the Christian era. Apparently the Christian era was simply the brief two thousand years during which the brainwashing of people to think of themselves as components of some fictitious entity reached its highest intensity. This ended in the atomic wars. The scholars who favor the Christian era dating system are much concerned that it be the one used. This apparently has to do with their belief in prophecy, a purported knowledge of what is going to happen before it happens. The fact that the full story as I learned it was made into an elaborate song-enactment over a hundred years before it happened seems to support the prophecy theory.

However, instead of prophecy, and instead of eras of dragon rule and heaven rule that alternate on a regular basis, I am inclined to agree with those scholars who say that there are two opposing man-made cultures that produce two radically different kinds of people. The opposing evolutionary directions of these two kinds of people make mortal conflict between them inevitable. Sometimes one side dominates the world for an extended period, sometimes the other. So there have been alternating periods of dragon rule and heaven rule that have happened over and over. Presumably, this will continue until one of the two opposing kinds of people is wiped out completely.

I think that it is important for everyone to know the kinds of events that trigger the repeating transitions between dragon and heaven rules, and to know the basic elements of the inevitable mortal conflict, so that each new born person can — consciously — choose sides.

I got the full continuity of my information regarding this kind of events from actually hearing a singing enactment of long past events as written down by a man named Wagner over a hundred years before another transition took place. It was an experience that no other person I have ever met has had so I will describe it briefly.

The whole was somehow made onto flat discs which, when combined in a complex way with a mysterious contrivance, caused music to come forth of such beauty that no words could describe it. The old man who had preserved this marvel from the ages past took a liking to me and was very generous. There were four sets of these discs and he allowed me to listen to a full set in appreciation of only one year of my hunting for him and bringing the meat I killed to his table. I hunted for him for four years and so I was able to hear all four of what he called "the ring operas."

The singing was in a language called German but there were "librettos," little books, which had the words written down in both German and English side by side. Also the old man had written down his own memories of very similar events that took place in his lifetime — thus giving two versions.

I am young, strong, tireless, a very good hunter, and so I had much leisure during which this generous man, impressed with my scholarly ability to read English, allowed me to read these librettos, and his own version of the similar events, as much as I liked. During each year of work, before hearing the actual singing, I read both versions so often that the very similar stories merged and formed one identical story in my mind. I now remember merely the language and thought patterns used in their telling as the major distinction between them. However, this man, who was very, very old and had lived through the whole of the more recent events, supplied me with other facts from his personal knowledge. These I will now tell before beginning the full story in its wonderfully significant great detail.

The names of the people, places, semi-abstract concepts, and phantom entities, as told to me by the old man from his personal knowledge, were often different from those of the "ring operas," but they have merged in my mind. In order to emphasize the parallel and avoid confusion, I will usually use the same ones in both cases. For such complex semi-abstract concepts as Rhinegold — Wildgold; Tarnhelm — controlled political machine for brainwashing a people; Ring — Oscar; et cetera, I will use the word that I think can best be illuminated by the context.

The fictitious entities need some special explanation. It is difficult for us who have not been brainwashed to think of them as real entities. However I will try to give the general idea.

It is well known that we live on the northern of two great bodies of land called North and South America. There are bigger and more complexly shaped bodies of land on the other side of the world. After the first atomic war the brainwashed zombis on this side were conditioned to think of themselves as parts, or "citizens," of the giant, FASOLT (Federated American Society of Latin Territories). Those on the other side were conditioned to think of themselves as parts of another giant, FAFNER (Federated Asiatic Farming Nations Eternal Republic). These fictitious entities, FASOLT and FAFNER, were routinely spoken of as actually doing things, just as if they were real beings.

7

FASOLT and FAFNER are the only giants, nations, or bodies politic, that feature in the detailed story. Before the first atomic war there were many such phantoms which existed only in the minds of the brainwashed people.

Some people still refer to the giants, or nations, as if these phantom entities could actually think and talk to each other. Some old people still talk about what happened as if these phantom entities actually existed and actually did the fighting. Wagner's version is geared to the thought pattern of these people.

In the events similar to the ones Wagner described, that happened in the old man's lifetime, the two giants that feature in the story were created in the minds of the people — as replacements for the many giants that the people believed previously existed — somewhere near the year 2000 of the Christian era.

During the same period, there developed a strong movement to reject all fictitious entities and their assumed sovereignty over individuals, and to recognize sovereignty — the ability to will and take action triggered by one's will — only in real, organic individuals. In the language of those who oriented on the Christian era, the transition from dragon rule to heaven rule, was spoken of as rejecting "the age of group-entities" and moving into the "new age of individual sovereignty."

The new people who commited to individual sovereignty were, for the most part, born in the cities but they rejected city life. They moved to the country areas and grew their own food but they did not become "farmers." Farmers grew food as a coin of commerce with the establishment. (Establishment was a word referring to the total conglomerate of those who still thought of themselves as parts of bodies politic, giants, or nations.) The new people grew food only for themselves. They wanted no commerce. They wanted detachment from what they called "the brainwashed zombis." They refused to relate to the establishment.

Whether called a transition period from dragon rule to heaven rule, a transition from "the age of group-entities" to the "new age of individual sovereignty," or something else, clearly something was happening. Attention, however, was distracted from the new people because the whole establishment became violently upset by what were called "civil disturbances" and "gang warfare."

"Civil disturbances" and "gang warfare" were terms used to distinguish between two different ways that the brainwashing of zombis was loosing its former effectiveness.

"Civil disturbance" was a phrase that meant organized fighting by people who had been fully conditioned to believe in, and respect, the general idea of nations, but were acting upon a newly developed dislike for the specific nation that claimed them as its component parts.

"Gang warfare" meant organized fighting by people whose conditioning had been only complete enough to confuse their instinctual perception of life's meaning, and had not been complete enough to instill respect for nations.

After the first atomic war, which killed at least nine-tenths of the people of the world, the new people were clearly recognized as different from all others, a difference that was conspicuous because of their ability to re-examine themselves and set a new long-range purpose. They diametrically reversed the old values of group worship. They emphasized protecting the individual from the group, and their culture was not simple lip service to individualism.

They made agreements among themselves that severely limited the acceptable use of group force. They agreed that individuals could be put to death by the group's decision to use group force if found guilty of murder, mayhem, rape, forceful sexual perversion, sexual abuse of children, or of secretly restraining other individuals. They agreed on conditions for settling matters outside the agreed use of group force by individual mortal combat. They viewed any group of two or more individuals who tried to extend the use of group force as an enemy to be destroyed as quickly as possible, and viewed all actions against such an enemy, by either individuals or groups, to be justified self defense or defense of individual sovereignty. Their declared purpose was individual sovereignty and they called themselves sovereigns.

The people of the establishment, meanwhile, had become even more dependent on group thinking and group cohesion for their survival. They now lived exclusively in small reconstructed cities, ate only synthetic food, abandoned all the areas that had been used for agriculture, and called everyone not within the cities "wildspeople."

To the establishment people everything outside their cities was outside the livable world. They exiled their criminals to the wilds instead of putting them in jails or executing them. This practice tended to actually make the wilds unlivable. Those exiled organized raids on the cities and used the establishment's manufactured articles, which they took in the raids, to buy their survival in the wilds. Soon a thriving commerce between semi-criminal elements in the cities and the exiles developed, with wildsmaidens as the other side of the commerce. The exiled criminals took captured wildsmaidens into the cities for use in brothels, as combination slaves and objects of sexual amusement, and sometimes for the simple purpose of breeding new children to be turned into zombis. The people in the cities had distorted their sexual instincts into perverted sensual amusements to such an extent that the steadily declining population was disturbing them.

The sovereigns took up arms against both the establishment's exiled criminals and the gangs in the cities that were dealing with these elements in the wilds. The fights were almost full scale warfare before the cities made laws declaring an instant death penalty for anyone outside the cities found in possession of any explosive or any weapon for firing an explosive. They enforced this with massed detachments of soldiers and ruthless zeal. Soon knives and the hunter's bow were the only weapons left to the wildspeople.

The second atomic war brought no new qualitative changes but did have a conspicuous effect. The cities lost a much higher proportion of population than the wilds in the bombings, the birthrate continued much higher in the wilds; so there was a growing relative number of sovereigns. They were becoming a world power.

Although there were no new differences the old differences between the establishment and the sovereigns were emphasized.

In the establishment, each reconstructed city had only the momentum of old habit to keep it functioning but the old east and west power groups still existed because they had differences of language and segregated systems of what were called TV networks. TV's were almost unbelievable devices for viewing things all over the world by all the people at the same time. The things shown to the zombis, however, were often deliberate distortions of what was happening because each of the two TV networks tried by distortion of things to make its own phantom entitiy, FASOLT or FAFNER, appear better than that of its rival. A feeling of rivalry between groups, considered as group-entities, was the basic factor of zombi brainwashing and now watching TV had become virtually the whole of life to the zombis.

The vast lands once used for agriculture and now abandoned became like primordial wild lands. There were fish, game, and edible plants in abundance. In the opinion of the sovereigns, the

10

atomic wars were miracles restoring man to the paradise that was his before he had been brainwashed. The real shift of power to the sovereigns came a little later but already it was possible to see the dawn of heaven rule.

The situation began to move toward a climax in the power shift when a young sovereign leader, who, to avoid the confusion of different names, I will call Wotan, became the hero of a TV program in the western federation of cities (FASOLT). This program blamed the eastern federation (FAFNER) for all of Wotan's difficulties in trying to make a world built on his ideals. FASOLT's propaganda claimed that the highly individualistic sovereigns led by Wotan derived their love of freedom from the old traditions of one of the original phantom giants, or bodies politic, call UNITED STATES, and so, in effect, were perpetuating and refining FASOLT's ideals. The program was called *"Men Like Gods."* As the name implied it glorified Wotan's daring and individualism in his forest exploits.

Too late the zombis discovered that Wotan was not just another controllable propaganda gimmick; he turned a portion of their own propaganda back against them. (Proaganda signifies a method for getting control of people through the clever use of words; it is one of the beginning stages of brainwashing.)

Wotan brought a new vocabulary into being. He called the bodies politic "teras," a word meaning monsters. He played heavily on the meaning of the word "zombi," which was the old word of the sovereigns for establishment people. He replaced the word "citizen" (a word that the zombis had been conditioned to think of with a favorable emotion) with "segment," sometimes "tera-segment," to emphasize that establishment individuals were mere pieces of something else and could not be considered as having individual existence. When considered as entities in themselves, as they had to be when banished into the wilds, he called the zombis "dwarfs," to indicate that their life as segments had given them small distorted souls.

Wotan's ideologies got into the cities through the "underground" and developed the high appeal of the forbidden. Adventure fads sprang up among groups of young people in the cities who sometimes banded into cults and went out to live "as gods" in the wilds. Many died from exposure, inexperience with wild animals, unfamiliarity with organic foods, or became quickly discouraged and returned to the cities. Sometimes they were killed by the hunters of the wilds and this fanned the existing ill feeling.

Inevitably the contacts between the two incompatible lifestyles developed into large scale organized hostility. Then the people of the cities set out to regain control over the people of the wilds.

In their first attempt they simply sent out bombers to reduce population by exterminating all who refused to recognize the historical authority of the teras. Here Wotan's status as a hero of TV programs came to his aid. A great cry on his behalf arose within the cities and grew into a loud popular demand that the United Nations (a separate army that was supposed to stop the nation-people from fighting each other) defend Wotan. Officially the teras ridiculed the idea, saying that the people of the wilds were not an organized nation and so, of course, not members of the United Nations. But Donner, the Chief of the United Nations as it was reorganized after the first atomic war, commanded a punitive bombing force sufficient to wipe out every city on earth. He studied his general orders, orders written when lip service was still accorded individual freedom, commanded the cities to desist and, when they did not, destroyed five of them. He was then ordered to resign. However he had a lifetime appointment. So he refused. He then found that he had become an outlaw with a capacity to destroy the whole world.

What direction the world affairs might have taken if Donner had been a fanatical molder of destinies is difficult to contemplate. However his temperament was that of a soldier; he looked for someone qualified to command him. An outlaw in the eyes of the establishment, he naturally turned to the sovereigns.

In return for certain public humanitarian promises and declarations from Wotan, Donner swore formal allegiance to him and placed his entire bombing force at Wotan's disposal. Donner, thus became a sovereign, and his power gave Wotan a bargaining position with the teras. Because the cities were much more vulnerable to bombing than his scattered sovereign hunters, the power between the total establishment and the sovereigns came into close balance.

This new equalization of power enables us to see the conflict in the wills and actions of only a few individuals that can easily be described.

Describing the events in the lives of these few individuals, brings into sharp focus the long standing conflict between the two kinds of people — the worldwide conflict in which every individual must either consciously choose sides, or else be swept into one

12

side or the other unthinkingly.

Wagner's version of the more ancient events was designed to portray, in a stage enactment, the conflict as it appears in the archetypal images of the subconscious. Before written words were invented, when all history was told in simplified verbal stories or songs, subconscious images were the ones generally used. Subconscious archetypal portrayals of this kind are now used primarily in drawn "cartoons."

I have written my version of the more recent events in current language, but I have included some of the thought patterns that the people just before the atomic wars had been conditioned, or "educated," to admit into their waking consciousness. I have done this because some of these conditioned thought patterns are still in common use.

I will set Wagner's "librettos" and my remembered version of the similar happenings, as written by the old man, side by side.

As I mentioned, language and thought patterns change from period to period. By comparing the two versions, future peoples, with completely new thought patterns, may be able to understand the kind of events that trigger repeated transitions from dragon rule to heaven rule — and also trigger the reversed transitions.

It is my hope that they will be able to see that the two kinds of people are unreconcilable mortal enemies because their ideals, and willed evolutionary directions, are in diametrical opposition. Therefore, these two kinds of people will cause the transitions to continually alternate, and continually create worldwide confusion, as long as these two different kinds of people continue to deal with each other as if they were a single species.

The archetypal thoughts that come from the subconscious, as shown by Wagner's version, already view the two kinds of people as beings of radically different species — and view any imagined matings between them as a repulsive and unacceptable perversion. In order to take sides by consciously identifying with one's own kind, everyone needs to bring these subconscious thoughts out for examination by his waking consciousness.

* * *

I will now change my focus from that of broad statements to the individual incidents that both symbolize and exemplify the comprehensive ideological struggle.

When I think of these things I actually see them in my mind, and that seems good, so I will tell everything now as if you could actually look at the things I tell and hear the people talk.

FIRST SCENE

At the bottom of the Rhine
A greenish twilight, lighter above than below. The upper part is filled with undulating water, which streams from right to left. Towards the bottom the waters resolve themselves into a fine mist, so that the space to a man's height from the stage seems free from water, which floats like a train of clouds over the gloomy space below. Steep rocky peaks jut up from the depths and enclose the whole stage. The bottom is a wild confusion of jagged rocks, while on all sides darkness indicates still more confusing gloom.

Around a rock, in the center of the stage, Woglinde circles with graceful swimming movements.

WOGLINDE. Weia! Waga! Roll you waters. Rock my cradle. Wagalawia!

WELLGUNDE. *(from above)* Woglinde, you guard the Rhinegold alone?

WOGLINDE. If Wellgunde joins me, there will be two.

WELLGUNDE. *(diving down near Woglinde)* How goes your watch? *(She tries to grab Woglinde.)*

WOGLINDE. *(swimming off to elude Wellgunde)* I'm able to dodge you. *(They playfully chase each other.)*

I

At the edge of the forest the ocean waves break on a smooth beach of white sand gleaming in the morning sun. Flat rocks waist high to higher than the head, rocks that would be covered at high tide, are now clean-washed and the sun has already dried them. Long white breakers roll in from the endless expanse of ocean. A young girl, Bingee, in scant leather sunsuit is playing in the surf. Her body movements say that it seems to her that the ocean is making love to her with its sensuousness. She in turn makes love to the ocean with the gift of her whole body, with her outstretched arms, and with the caressing, inviting tone she works at injecting into meaningless words and snatches of song that she repeats over and over with new experiments of intonation.

Kristi, another girl similarly dressed in leather, has been stretched out unseen on a high flat rock. She now sits up and watches, vicariously enjoying the mood of the younger girl. She voices her participation by calling out, "You've found a mighty strange lover." The other girl turns and waves at her words then goes back to her play. Kristi stands up, stretches and enfolds the air in her arms, then again watches Bingee. "Hold him tight," she calls. "Wotan said we must watch carefully to keep someone from stealing our ocean."

Bingee waves again at Kristi's words, then turns back, waits for an oncoming wave, takes it in her arms, kisses it goodby, then runs back through the water toward Kristi. She makes experimental dance motions with the exuberance of her youth as she questions the older girl with the searching seriousness of her adolescence: "What does Wotan mean by that? It doesn't make sense to me. He said we must let no one *steal* from us the ocean and the mountains and the sun and the stars. I don't understand."

Kristi is in no hurry to answer. She jumps down, stretches, does a cartwheel, stretches again, gives her face, her open mouth and her whole body to the rays of the sun. Being satisfied and ready to let the answer come from her whole being, she speaks at last, half communing with her memories: "You'll understand some day. In the arms of my lover I lose the ocean and the mountains. The warmth of his body is my sun and the only stars

15

FLOSSHILDE. *(calling from above)* Helaha weia! Watch out, you wild sisters!

WELLGUNDE. Flosshilde, join me! Woglinde is flying. Help me to catch and hold her.

FLOSSHILDE. *(dives down and comes between them.)* You're pretty lax in guarding the Rhinegold. If you don't watch more carefully, you may pay dearly for your carelessness.

(In contradiction to her serious words, Flosshilde joins the other two in a playful game of tag. Flosshilde chases first one, then the other. They dodge her and then join together in trying to catch her. All dodge about chasing each other while they shout defiance with jests and laughter. From the dark cavern, Alberich clambers up on one of the rocks. He pauses in the shadows and watches the Rhine-maiden's joyful play with vicarious pleasure.)

ALBERICH. Hey, hey! You nixes! You are a lovely new folk. Coming from Nibelhelm's night, I would like to join you if you would be kind and let me.

(Hearing Alberich's voice, the Rhine-maidens immediately stop playing.)

WOGLINDE. Hei! Who is there?

WELLGUNDE. A thing with an awful voice.

FLOSSHILDE. Let's see what thing is below!

(They all dive and see the Nibelung.)

WOGLINDE and WELLGUNDE. Fie! What a loathsome thing!

FLOSSHILDE. *(swimming up quickly)* Let's guard the Rhinegold! Father warned us of such a foe.

(The other two follow her, and all three gather quickly around the central rock.)

ALBERICH. Hey, you up above there.

THE THREE RHINE-MAIDENS. What do you want from down below?

ALBERICH. Do I spoil your fun just by watching you? If you would just come nearer, a poor Nibelung would like to join in your play.

WOGLINDE. Can he only wish to join us?

I can see are those in his eyes."

"*That's* not what he means. You're playing with me. You're always playing with me. And you're *confusing* me. Wotan warned against a *substitute* for love. Wotan upholds love and lovers as the things *most* needing protection from the teras."

A third girl, Inger, comes from behind a tall rock, caressing it with her hands and body as she slides around it so as to enjoy its texture. "But who for love would not gladly give the world?" she asks.

Bingee persists, "Wotan didn't say anything about trading the world for love. He said to guard against a thief who would steal the world."

Kristi offers, "But the thief is subtle and plays clever underhanded games. He plays games with love. It is to recognize such a thief when we meet one that he told us to be on our guard."

A voice causes them to turn and see, coming across the beach, a young but unattractive man in ridiculous bathing garb. He calls, "Hey, there, I'll bet you can persuade me to vacation with you if you'll throw some of your charms my way."

Bingee reacts first, makes a face expressing revulsion, and says, "What a horrible voice."

"That's the kind of voice that could belong to a thief," Kristi adds.

Inger runs across the sand toward the intruder as if she would head him off and protect the others, "Who are *you* and what do you want here?"

Bingee and Kristi, left behind, exchange words of mock wonder, "Ugh, what can it be — that loathsome thing?" "Do you think it could really be a man?"

Inger slows to let the others catch up and warns them, "Watch yourselves. This might really be the sort of enemy we were to guard against accepting."

The young man, Alber, ogles the girls ostentatiously and says, "Real luscious. All of you."

"What do you *want* here?" comes again from the wildsmaidens.

"Cool it kids, cool it. Don't get excited now. I'm not going to hurt you. I'm just looking over the country and the people. Could be it has possibilities. I might take it in hand, you know. I might make something of this lousy place. But right now I'm just relaxing. I just want to play around a little. Kind of get acquainted."

Kristi, to the other girls, with faint sarcasm: "He just wants

17

WELLGUNDE. Is he making some kind of joke?

ALBERICH. How sweet and soft you look in this light! If you'd just come down, I'd gladly hold you in my arms.

FLOSSHILDE. I now laugh at my fears. Our enemy is in love with us. *(All laugh.)*

WELLGUNDE. That mooning calf!

WOGLINDE. *(She goes down lower on the rock, near where Alberich has approached to its base.)* Let's speak to him.

ALBERICH. She's coming down!

WOGLINDE. Climb up here to me.

ALBERICH. *(clambers with gnome-like rapidity, but with difficulty, higher up on the rock.)* This stone's all smooth with slippery slime. My hands and feet can't get any hold on it. *(He sneezes.)* It's clammy here, too, and brings on my sneezes. *(He has got near to Woglinde.)*

WOGLINDE. The sound of sneezing announces the arrival of my suitor.

ALBERICH. Come on, be mine, my beautiful child! *(He tries to take her in his arms.)*

WOGLINDE. *(slipping away from him)* If you want to make love, then follow me here. *(She quickly moves to another rock. The other Rhine-maidens laugh.)*

ALBERICH. How can I capture someone as fleet as a fish? *(He tries to climb after her.)*

WOGLINDE. *(diving down into the depths)* Come on down here and you can catch me.

ALBERICH. *(scrambling down)* Much better down lower.

WOGLINDE. *(darting quickly up to a high peak at the side)* But look, I'm now up here.

ALBERICH. *(trying to get up)* You're a timid sort of fish!

to play with us. Now isn't that sweet."

Inger, with sarcasm intended to be heard and clearly interpreted: "Play? Him play? He wouldn't know how to play. He's got to be kidding."

"Come a little closer," he says, "and I'll show you. I can show you some new kind of play that you've never thought of."

"With this thing here," Inger ridicules, talking to the other girls as if he were not there, "we can forget our fears. We were to guard against establishment dwarfs offering a substitute for love."

"Sure, this thing looks like a lovesick frog," Kristi injects. She is pleased by the insult of talking about him in his presence as if he were an inhuman object.

"Let's see if he's real," Bingee takes up the attitude and makes a gesture as if to poke him.

The man's voice grates in its inept attempt to be seductive, "Come on, kid, give me your hand."

Bingee reaches her hand almost to him, then draws back luringly as he follows. "Let's go play in the surf," she invites, and easily evades as he chases her, stumbling and adjusting his clothes.

Soon he stops and slouches his shoulders in an elaborate expression of exhaustion. "Aw, take it easy. I haven't got the patience for this kind of play. I'm a big time wheeler-dealer, the sort of guy who has what he wants brought to him. I can't waste time like this."

Enjoying her play with the two older girls as her audience, Bingee stops and acts out for them a mock gesture of swooning. "The stumbling of weak feet and the sound of feeble panting tells me that my suitor comes."

"Wait for me, you slippery little eel," he calls to her as he resumes the chase.

She springs lightly on a boulder and invites, "Here, come and catch me if you want to make love."

He scrambles up the rock after her and she leaps to another when almost within his grasp. He pauses, "Aw, come off it. This is going too far. You are as hard to grab onto as your people's dumb ideas and crazy language."

"Come on; there's nowhere I can go from here."

Instead of leaping to the other rock, he climbs down, stumbles across, and looks for a foothold helplessly. He holds out his arms, "Here, jump down and I'll catch you."

WELLGUNDE. *(has moved to a low rock on the other side.)* Heia! My dashing hero! Give me your attention.

ALBERICH. *(turning around)* You're talking to me?

WELLGUNDE. Forget Woglinde. I'm here for you, if you want real play.

ALBERICH. *(clambering over the rocks toward her)* And more beautiful, too, you are, than that sleek sly one. But you need to come closer.

WELLGUNDE. *(coming nearer to him)* So now I am closer.

ALBERICH. Not close enough. Put your tender arms around me, and let me fondle your enticing body in a panting embrace.

WELLGUNDE. Are you really in love and longing for favors? Well, let me see what recommends you to me. Urp! You swarthy, horned skinned, shrivelled up dwarf! If you want to make love, hunt up a mate of your own kind!

ALBERICH. *(trying to hold her by force)* I may not look so good, but I take what I want.

WELLGUNDE. *(easily escaping and swimming up to the central rock)* You need to hold me better than that.

(The Rhine-maidens all laugh.)

ALBERICH. *(calling angrily after her)* You fickle chit! You chilly, slippery fish! If I don't seem shapely, and tenderly enticing, then go and make love with the eels!

FLOSSHILDE. Don't get upset now, dwarf. You have only tried your luck with two. But with a third one a soft reward surely awaits you.

ALBERICH. Your words make beautiful music. Where there are many to choose from, one among the many must find me delightful. But before I believe you are the one, you must come closer and show me.

FLOSSHILDE. *(dives down to Alberich.)* How foolish you are, my sisters, not to be awed by his grace and charm!

"*You* couldn't catch me. I'd knock you sprawling like a crab."
Her audience laughs appreciatively at the possibility.

Her pursuer struggles for a hold on the rock without success.
"There must be some way to get next to you. Wait for me now;
I'm coming up."

Kristi leaps to another rock, stretches herself, displaying her
beautiful body as she calls, "Hey there, my mating frog."

Alber, glad to abandon the frustrating climb, turns and says,
"What, do you want to play too?"

"Sure. You give her up. She's too young and love shy. Come
up here to me."

"You are much prettier too than that little sprite. I like my
women a little more rounded. But you must come closer."

"I'm close."

"Not close enough. I need the touch of smooth skin and the
pneumatic pressure of young flesh."

"I think you try to talk about love but you don't do it well.
Never mind. Come and show me your face and form. If you are
strong and handsome words aren't necessary." He comes closer
and takes a deep breath as if expanding with passion. She leans
over and examines him from the rock above as if he were some
strange specimen of sea life. "Ugh. What an unhealthy looking,
ghoulish creature. How can a dwarf as swarthy and horn-skinned
as you remind me of the underbelly of a toad?" She draws back.
"Go find yourself a sweetheart with a taste for dank coarseness.
You're not for me."

He grabs her ankle and exclaims triumphantly, "I may not
attract but I take what I want."

"Ha! Now the lovesick toad is a bold conqueror." She jerks
her foot loose, plants it in his face and sends him sprawling. The
new two-girl audience applauds the new performer.

Alber picks himself up and glares at Kristi, "Fickle aren't
you? You live too damn freely out here in the wilds. But you will
be tamed. And all your people with you. Meanwhile give your
love to your damned gods — or wild devils they'd be better named."

Inger now seeks her turn. "What's this, dwarf? Daunted so
soon? You've wooed two and lost, but a third still waits to soothe
your hurts with caresses."

"At last now a *real* dish. Come over here and show me your
willing worth."

Inger approaches him in mock admiration. "How insensitive

ALBERICH. *(hurrying toward her)* Both of them are dull and hideous by comparison to you.

FLOSSHILDE. Sing on. Your words are music to my ears.

ALBERICH. *(caressing her)* My heart flutters and falls at the sound of your flattering words.

FLOSSHILDE. *(gently resisting him)* Your beauty gladdens my vison, and your tender smile dispels my fears. *(She draws him to her.)* Most wonderful of men!

ALBERICH. Sweetest of maidens!

FLOSSHILDE. If you were only mine!

ALBERICH. If you were mine forever!

FLOSSHILDE. *(holding him quiet in her arms)* Oh! Your beady eyes, and horn skinned face, just to see and fondle them with tenderness. To have your straggled hair floating around Flosshilde for ever and ever. You are so toad like, and talk in such a croaking tone, Oh! How could I help but marvel on all these forever!

(Woglinde and Wellgunde have dived down near them and now burst out with uncontainable laughter.)

ALBERICH. *(starting with alarm)* Do you all dare laugh at me!

FLOSSHILDE. *(suddenly throwing him aside)* And so ends our love song. *(She goes with her sisters and joins in the laughter.)*

ALBERICH. *(in a screaming voice)* Woe is me! Ah, woe is me. The third one also was laughing at me. All shocking, shifty, shameless wantons! Doesn't any of your brood know anything about faithfulness?

THE THREE RHINE-MAIDENS. Walala! Lalala! Lale! Heia! Heia! Heia! Shame on you, dwarf, to fume and do nothing. How can such a mooning calf hope to hang on to the lady of his love? True are we to one with arms strong enough to hold us. Don't stand still and hurl words at us. Grab us! Where can we go but here in the waves? *(They swim about, around and around, high and low, trying to incite the dwarf to chase them.)*

you silly girls are not to see him as he really is!''

Hastening toward her he tries to get close but not to scare her away by touching her. "I can only think of them as dull and unattractive now that I see you."

"Sing on. At least the words of your song are the kind I like to hear."

He touches her and when she doesn't pull away begins to caress her with confidence. "Now this is more as it should be: A smart girl who knows what a man likes."

Gently avoiding his touch she covers her repulsion to let him interpret her words as applying to him. "Masculine strength and rugged beauty thrill the depths of my being. A tender smile calms all fears and doubts that rise up within me."

"You like it, huh?"

She draws him toward her to explore in imagination the depths of her repulsion. "What would it be like if *you* were mine?"

"You'll find out. Now. I'll make you mine and quickly."

He tries to pull her toward him and she pulls back a little as if only to admire, meanwhile playing with the horror of her imagination and saying in mock ardor, "To look into your non-understanding eyes, to feel your weak arms about me, or to listen to your rasping voice declaring the emotions of a croaking frog. You doubtless think I could marvel on these forever."

Coming closer, the other girls try to hold straight faces but can't contain their laughter at her sport. It bursts in a torrent.

Alber starts back in alarm. "You little chits. You dare to keep laughing at me?"

As if coming out of a horrible nightmare of self-hypnotic making, Inger shudders and runs over to join the other girls as she says, "And so ends our love song."

They feel the intensity of the mood she created by momentarily submitting herself to physical contact, but they appreciate her performance and applaud it with their laughter and dancing.

Alber's anger and frustration cause his voice to take on an even less assured and more wailing rasp. "Damn you little bitches, you gods, or sovereigns, or whatever the hell you call yourselves. No damned morals at all, but nobody can ever figure you." They have moved away and begun playing with improvised dance steps to explore for themselves their own moods after the experience. He shouts his last words, "Get lost then if you want to keep living like worthless tramps!"

After dancing and singing wordless songs they again find

ALBERICH. A mix up of love and rage burns through my whole body like a destructive fire. But the fire raises my pulses and increases my strength. So you three can laugh and lie your fill — one of you I must have and you may be sure I'll get you! *(He chases them with desperate energy. He clambers from rock to rock, springing after first one of the Rhine-maidens and then another. They always elude him with mocking laughter. At last he staggers and falls below. Out of breath, he can only shake his clenched fist at them.)*

ALBERICH. If this fist could only hold one! *(He remains speechless with rage. Gazing upward, he is attracted and his attention becomes rivetted on the following sight: Through the water above an ever-increasing glow comes from the top of the central rock. From something there, a magical golden light streams through and illuminates the water.)*

WOGLINDE. Look sisters! The wakener laughs in the deep.

WELLGUNDE. Through the dark green billows the sleeper alures us.

FLOSSHILDE. Kissing its eyelids in the effort to open them, bathed in splendor, it sends its glow through the surrounding waters like a whole stream of stars.

ALL THREE. *(swimming joyously around the rock)* Heia jaheia! Heia jahaia! Wallala la la la leia jahei! Rhinegold! Rhinegold! Lustrous delight! How glorious and glad your laughter goes out wide over the waves. Heiajahei! Heiajahei! Waken friend! Wake with joy! We know your playful games and we love to play them with you. Flashes in the foam, flames in the flood, all embrace us as we swim about dancing, diving and singing, as we blissfully bathe in your bed. Rhinegold! Rhinegold! Heiajahia! Walalaleia jahei!

themselves in the mood to confront him. "Shame on you, dwarf. You are the most fainthearted lover who ever came wooing. We love and are faithful to love beyond your wildest dreams. But we love men who are bold and sure, and strong enough to hold a woman when they love her. We are yet only children and even so you are not strong enough to hold us. Try again, fainthearted weak one." They dance about him on the beach and rocks, now near, now far, taunting him to give chase.

He stands in one place and glares at them. "You chits could lash a man's passion to madness. But my day is coming. Half the people of this area already have contracts with me. They are going to discover that those contracts mean more than they thought. And these stupid fools are faithful to their word until death. You'll see. They'll be crawling on their bellies to me just for a few crumbs of food. Just wait until I have control here. One or all of you I may want. And you can bet you'll come running when I snap my fingers."

He makes another quick effort, runs and chases them with the desperate energy of his frustrated passion. They elude and taunt him with mocking laughter. He stumbles and falls. They pretend to help him up but laughingly push him down and run again. At last he pauses out of breath, fuming with rage, and shakes a clenched fist at them. "Wait 'til I have you between four walls and the doors locked."

"Let's forget him," Bingee turns away. She dances down the beach then calls back, "Come on. The wind is blowing again in the forest above us. It's playing our favorite dance song."

Kristi listens, and comes back to the world they know. "The tide is coming in too. And the waves are getting higher."

Inger leads off resolutely. "Let's run down where the beach is smooth and dive in the waves as they rush at us. I like to feel their power as they tower above me and see the green light through them just before they break. I'm like Bingee: I feel that the waves are my lover."

Alber remains speechless with rage because the girls, tiring of their sport, have turned to no more replacement for him than their enjoyment of the breeze, the warm sun, and the dashing waves of the incoming tide.

They go off and forget him. As he watches from a distance they play in the surf together with increasing joy and abandon, making up a song to some tune he doesn't know: "Wildgold! Wildgold! Wildgold! A whole wide world of youth and freedom.

ALBERICH. *(whose eyes, fascinated by the light, beome fixed on the Rhinegold)* What is it, you dancers, that cause the gleam and glow?

THE THREE RHINE-MAIDENS. Where do you come from dwarf, that you know nothing of the Rhinegold?

WELLGUNDE. You know nothing of the bright glow that wakes and sleeps in turns?

WOGLINDE. You know nothing of the wonderous light that illumines the waves?

THE THREE RHINE-MAIDENS. See how joyously we blend in its radiance! If you, laggard, would like to know its joy, come join, play and swim with us. Wallala la la leia lalei! Wallala la la leia lalei!

ALBERICH. If what you prize highly, is good only for play, I have no interest in it.

WOGLINDE. You would not scoff at the Rhinegold if you knew all its wonders.

WELLGUNDE. The world as a kingdom one can win who from the Rhinegold fashions a Ring that gives power without measure.

FLOSSHILDE. Our father firmly told us to guard the Rhinegold with great care, for fear some thief might steal it from us. Be still, then, you chattering fools.

WELLGUNDE. No need to reprove us, prudent sister. Remember what qualities one must have before he can use the Rhinegold to fashion the ring's power.

WOGLINDE. Only one who denounces love can master the skill that molds the Rhinegold into the power of the ring.

WELLGUNDE. We're safe so long as such requirements hold, for surely no one can denounce the boundless worth of love.

After the world seen in the sick soul of that dwarf, our own wildworld is more wonderful still. Wildworld! Wildworld! Forest, sun, rocks, air, sand, waves. Joy and freedom. World of Wotan and Wotan's strong-armed warriors. Wildgold! Wildgold!''

Following them and seeking to discover the fascination that has drawn them from him, he asks in newly discovered unbelief, "What kicks do you get from that dirty sand and cold water?''

They answer him at brief pauses in their dancing:

"Is it really as Wotan says: Do you dwarfs from the cities no longer know the joys of freedom and play?''

"Does the beach truly seem to you dirty and repulsive? And do the waves seem cold and fearful?''

"Are you actually frightened by the green depths of the forest? And does a rushing mountain stream hold for you nothing but terror?''

"The men of our world have no fears. And they love with the force and passion of a breaking wave. Come on with us into the ocean if you would learn of love.''

He answers when they pause near him, "From the ocean your villagers get nothing but stinking fish. But from the ocean we dwarfs, as you call us, synthesize both food and metal wealth like you can't imagine.''

"We know. We have heard. And from the rocks and sands you make wondrous jewels and fine ornaments.''

"And from the forest you make beautiful cloth and many strange things. And the promise of all these wonders gives measureless power if one can control people's desire for them.''

Inger cautions Bingee and Kristi, "Wotan told all our people to guard against trading things as they are for the promise of things that could be made. Watch what you say to a man like this.''

Kristi discredits the caution, "No such dwarf as this needs to be dodged as something dangerous. I can't even imagine what the subtle thief of Wotan's warning would look like. No person we have ever met could fashion the lure that gives the dangerous power.''

"No,'' adds Bingee, repeating the facts she has been told. "to do it one has to devote himself wholly to the boring job. He must sleep little and scheme every waking hour. He must think of nothing but manipulating people and their desire for wealth. He must even forswear love.''

"We are safe,'' Kristi reinforces. "The dwarfs who wield this power over their kind are of a different species from any we've

WOGLINDE. This dwarf least of all, whose lustful rage will surely be his death.

FLOSSHILDE. I have no fear of him. I was close enough to almost be burned by his raging lust.

WOGLINDE. He is like a brimstone brand making our cool water hiss with his lust rage.

ALL THREE. Walalaleia! Lahei! Loathsome dwarf, through the golden gleam you look lovely. Come, lovely one, join in our laughter. Heia jaheia! Heia jaheia! Wallala la la la jahei! *(Laughing, they swim backwards and forwards in the light.)*

ALBERICH. *(with his eyes rivetted on the Rhinegold, has listened closely to the Rhine-maiden's talk.)* Could I really gain the world as my kingdom? Without love another delight could be mine. *(Terribly loud.)* Mock away! Mock away! The Nibelung makes for your toy! *(Raging, he springs on the central rock and clambers to the summit. The Rhine-maidens separate screaming and dart upwards in different directions.)*

ALL THREE. Heia! Heia! Heiahahei! Save us all! The dwarf is insane! The water spurts where he springs. He is made mad with his kind of love.

ALBERICH. *(at the summit of the central peak, stretching out his hand toward the Rhinegold)* Do you fear me now? You can play in the darkness. The light's luster I quench as I rend from the rock the Rhinegold. Vengeance I'll wreak with the Ring, for, hear me, you floods — Love I forswear forever.

(With terrible strength, he tears the Rhinegold from the rock and hastily disappears below. Sudden darkness overspreads the scene. The Rhine-maidens dive down after the robber.)

ever seen. They couldn't hide among Wotan's warriors. They couldn't even hide among the degenerating villagers.''

Bingee: "Certainly this love-sick dwarf, chasing every girl he sees, is not the kind who could wield such power.''

"I'm not afraid of him,'' says Inger. It's the tone of envy in your voices when you talk of his possible wealth that disturbs me.''

"Don't be afraid because he hears what we say. He was doubtless cast out from the cities because of his crude love. It must be that crazy mixed-up love-distorted madness they call lust.''

This last from Kristi seems to satisfy Inger. She changes attitude and they approach Alber, agreed in their thoughts again and wholly without fear. They even return to their normal fellow-feeling for all forms of life.

"Join us in our play and laughter, lovesick dwarf. You could not forswear love and become a leader of your kind. But don't feel bad about it. There are much better things. Maybe you can forswear you lust for power and learn something of real love. Come on. Face the test. Become a god or die.'' They dance around and motion to him to join them in the waves of the ocean.

Not sensing their change of mood, he fumes again. "Mock *me*, will you, you little pagans. Like the fools who signed them you don't know what it means that I have contracts with half your people that will make them my slaves inch by inch. Your love I may not win but by cunning I'll have my delight in you.''

They return to their mocking tone and move away. "Let's save ourselves! The dwarf who can't even hold a child babbles of his power. He's mad for possessions. Beware, he will have us!''

He turns away, then pauses, reaches in the folds of his garb and pulls forth a long, glittering, link-chain necklace. He holds it out to them. "Here, take this, and know that I will make your sea and your forest yield up mountains more that will make this look dowdy by comparison.''

They recoil as if the necklace were a dangerous weapon. He throws it on the sand and swaggers away.

The wildsmaidens back away from the glittering thing at their feet.

Then Kristi comes back. She picks it up gingerly and examines it.

Bingee and Inger both come up and all examine it. Becoming bolder, they run the heavy links through their fingers and hold it up to the light.

THE THREE RHINE-MAIDENS. Hinder the robber. Rescue the Rhinegold. Help us. Help us. Woe! Woe!

Suddenly, Inger seizes it and throws it toward the surf. She cries in horror, "It *is* the thief! It's the subtle thief of Wotan's warning! It's the one that works so hard at appearing harmless. He begins by giving you something then takes away everything that you have."

Staring at the necklace, they stand frozen in wonder and unbelief, then, as a wave threatens to cover it, Kristi rushes forward and grabs it. She examines it again hesitatingly for a moment, then admiringly winds it around her wrist and dances hesitatingly. Then she tries it about her waist and dances with more confidence. At last she winds it around her neck and dances with total abandon. Meanwhile, Inger and Bingee have watched, first in horror, then interest, and at last have approached and watched with envy.

"Take this, and know that I will make your sea and your forest
yield up mountains more."

SECOND SCENE

Gradually the waves give place to clouds, then fine mist, clearing to show:

An open space on a mountain top.

Dawning day lights, with increasing brightness, a castle with glittering pinnacles, which stands on a cliff in the back. Between this and the foreground is a deep valley through which the Rhine is supposed to flow. At one side Wotan and Fricka are lying asleep in a flowery meadow.

FRICKA. *(wakes, and her eyes fall on the castle. She starts in surprise.)* Wotan! My lord! Awaken!

WOTAN. *(still dreaming)* The happy hall of delight is guarded by gate and gulf. Manhood's honor, and honor's power, rise to the pinnacle of fame!

FRICKA. *(shaking him)* Wake from your vain and rosy visions! Wake up, my husband, wake up and consider!

34

II

The room is large and well designed but made without precision tools. It is the study of Wotan's house from which he administers his organization and armies in the wilds. In the center of the room is a massive rough-hewn council table, and heavy, hand-made chairs. There is a massive stone fireplace to the right. To the rear a large window looks out across a river to the view of a city on a hill.

The contrast between the view from the room's window and the room's interior is striking. It is the contrast between two worlds. The city, as yet totally uninhabited, was designed and built as a single unit for impressive appearance. It contains materials and workmanship of the finest the world has ever known. The room represents Wotan's world.

Wotan, mature and dignified, but still a young man, sits at the table dreamily gazing at the glittering city. His clothes are brown leather with dark brown belt and boots. He wears a short sword (bayonet size) at his belt. His clothes are trim and well-fitted; the belt has a brass buckle; there are brass buttons and ornaments on coat and shoulders; everything gives him a military appearance.

Fricka, his wife, moves about the room impatiently. She is young but matronly in speech and mannerisms. Her clothes are cloth of inconspicuous design but with some tendency toward regality in cut and ornamentation. She stops in her pacing and faces Wotan squarely as she says, "Wotan! Wake up! Stop dreaming and look at reality."

He remains absorbed in his thoughts and only slowly returns to the world of her confrontation.

"There is a difference between dreaming and planning," he says. "I have now gained prestige for my ideals in the eyes of those who respect ideals only if accompanied by tangible grandeur. That is much."

"You are dreaming still," she answers with an edge of scorn. "You deceive yourself by concentrating only on advantages. Consider the whole."

WOTAN. *(wakes and raises himself slightly. His eyes are at once attracted and held by the sight of the castle.)* It is finished — the enormous work. On yonder summit a home for the gods proudly rears its radiant strength. As I visioned and ordered it, strong it stands, a grand and glorious structure.

FRICKA. So you welcome the thing that I view with dread? Your castle is fine but I fear for Freia. Pause and remember the price that must be paid. Your castle is finished and now you must meet the contract. Have you no care for the cost?

WOTAN. I well remember the bargain I made with them who built this burg. My agreement held them in check while this hallowed hall they built for me. It stands — the work they accomplished for me. You don't need to worry about its cost.

FRICKA. Look now, at your laughing lightness. If I had but known what was in the contract this horrible result might have been avoided. But you failed to consider a woman's point of view. Alone you bargained with the giants. Now, without shame, you plan to give them my glorious sister, Freia. Nothing remains holy to men who pant for power.

WOTAN. Was your yearning any the less holy — your greed for this castle?

FRICKA. I wanted something to hold you to me when you tended to stray afield. Halls high and stately, gleaming with splendor, were seen as something to allure you to stay beside me in peaceful repose. But you saw this castle as something that added to your power and might. You viewed it only as an addition to your power.

Wotan leans back and relaxes as he answers, "The lure of the cities will be less great now that we sovereigns have a city equal to any that the teras claim. Also private atomic planes for all our staff and commanders are part of the agreement. Most effective of all will be our own television broadcasts with open air receiving theaters scattered throughout the world. Our rise to a world power was helped immeasurably by FASOLT's TV program *Men Like Gods*. With our own broadcasts the possibilities are unlimited."

Fricka resumes her pacing. "You are still looking only at gain and forgetting the price. Promises to police the world and protect the cities from raids — raids led by their own outcasts — promises to permit the people of the cities freedom to go and come into our world, even promises to permit free trade and bargaining — these I can understand. But the treaties should contain some restrictions. They should prevent the teras from luring our women and young girls — children — into their cities."

Wotan responds, "I am fully aware of the terms of the bargain. Their race is dying and they want new blood which they hope to get. That's their main objective; now is not the time to make it an open issue. Also by the treaty they plan to restrict my freedom of action. But the advantage I gain is greater than I give. I can consolidate the scattered peoples of the wilds, easily overcome any organized opposition, and be in a position to beat the teras at their own game. We go either to total victory or total defeat. When everything is at stake only a fool will weigh separately each item of cost."

Fricka interrupts him, "Wotan! You are dreaming still. Or else you have a callous streak that I would hate to believe of you. If I had known the full terms of the bargain it would never have been made. Already the procurement of naive girls for the cities has become open enough to be scandalous. Knowing this, and that the treaty would only make it easier, you should have included agreements to prevent it. If nothing remains sacred in your greed for power, you are no different from those of the establishment that you seek to displace."

Wotan's own thoughts are now fully disrupted. He stands up as he answers her, "Don't speak to me of greed. What but greed made you want the prestige and luxury of a city for the sovereigns?" He walks to the window and looks out over the city.

Fricka says, "I needed something to attract and keep you at home, something to divert the energy of the nomad and warrior

37

WOTAN. *(smiling)* Would you, O wife, confine me in a castle. To me, the god, must be granted, faithful at home, the opportunity to fight where I will. Ranging and changing is what all men love. This activity must not be taken from me.

FRICKA. Light-hearted, unloving, low-natured man! For the might to change, you would trample in contempt over love and a woman's worth!

WOTAN. *(earnestly)* When I sought to win you for a wife, my one eye I risked in a wager. I value women higher than you approve. I am not going to sacrifice Freia. That has never been my intention.

FRICKA. Then save her at once — defenseless and in fear, she's now coming to you for help.

FREIA. *(entering hastily)* Help me, sister! Save me, Wotan! Fasolt is coming from yonder mountain to take me captive!

WOTAN. Let him come. Have you seen Loge?

FRICKA. Why do you still trust that tricky deceiver? You have suffered enough at his hands. Why keep trusting him?

from finding outlet in fights and restless roving. I visioned stability and peace. But in your eyes our own city was only a lever giving you the power to wage greater war."

He answers her, "Man contributes the quality of his being to the world by his will to selective destruction. Woman contributes her part by attracting, cherishing, and protecting what she has chosen. Free yourself from the establishment's conditioned thought patterns; woman has no exclusive on morality. Creation by selective destruction is the function of man. The segments surrendered their combat selectiveness to the teras and so became less than men. From me, a sovereign, it must not be taken, neither by the bigness of the teras, who would absorb me, nor by the tender possessiveness of a woman who closes her eyes to all but love."

"For empire and sway, would you, in insolent scorn, stake love and a woman's worth?"

"Empire and sway is the game of teras and segments. I deal in realities. I recognize myself as one side of a two-sex system — a total divided into two parts. To love woman as a man I surrendered half of myself: male and female, combat and love, are two sides of our aboriginal oneness. As we increase our capacity for combat, just so, in equal measure, we must increase our capacity for love. I honor woman and love beyond your greatest desire, and I am not going to abandon them now. That was never my intention."

"Yet, even now," Fricka answers, "the wildsmaidens are being carried off in ever greater numbers. Already the teras feel themselves protected by the treaty and those who deal with their dwarf outcasts move more openly. Even in the Godsland we may well fear for our sisters and daughters."

Wotan says, "The wildsmaidens have always been lured or taken to the cities. It was going on before I was born. The warnings I have given them have done little good. I must beat the teras at their game of bidding for popular appeal. Such a game is not to my liking; I am a warrior. Have you seen Logi?"

Fricka whirls and faces him. "Why, against the evidence of all good sense, do you still trust that deceiver? Always he trips you up. Was it not he who advised you on the treaty that put Donner at your side, that gave you enough missiles to destroy the whole world but prohibited you by the same treaty from using them on the teras? Logi, himself, inserted the words that you would use no explosive unless there was an open break of treaty. The game played by the teras and segments is never played in the open. So they continue to destroy you by their underhanded methods, while

39

WOTAN. I ask no aid where men fight with honest weapons. But where my enemies fight with fraud, I can learn their way of fighting from Loge, who knows it. He advised me in this agreement and promised a way to extricate Freia. I am relying fully on him for this.

FRICKA. And again you are left in the lurch. Look now, the giants are already coming. And where is your ally lurking?

FREIA. Why don't my brothers come to help me when Wotan makes me something with which to bargain? Where are you, Donner? Come rescue me, Froh!

FRICKA. The ones who pushed you into this false bargain have now deserted you.

(Fasolt and Fafner, both of gigantic stature and armed with strong staves, enter.)

FASOLT. While soft sleep sealed your eyes, we were up laboring tirelessly, heaping up stones, building towers, and walls, and gates. There stands the fair fruit of our labor, bright in the beams of this day. It is ready for you to enter. So pay our wage.

WOTAN. Workmen, name your wage. What payment will satisfy you?

FASOLT. We agreed on the payment before the work had begun. You can't have forgotten. Freia, the fair one, and Holda, the free one, make up the payment. The bargain is that we now take them away.

your hands remain tied.''

Wotan: ''I ask no aid where simple truth is the language of men. But the teras know only legalities. Logi knows their legal jargon and twisted thoughts. And he assures me that from this bargain another can be made which will give us what we want.''

''And again he has left you in the lurch,'' Fricka says. ''The negotiators for the teras have already arrived. Their planes came in several minutes ago. Right now they are coming down the hall, being shown to your study. It is not only the wildsmaidens who are on the bargaining table along with your freedom. All sovereign women are on that bargaining table, too. Donner's hands are tied by your treaties and the knave who plotted and tricked you has hidden away on the day of reckoning.''

The door is opened by a guardsman who shows in the negotiators from FAFNER and FASOLT. They wear the conventional business suits of the era. The guard's dress is the same as Wotan's except that everything else but the dark brown boots, belt and sword sheath are forest green leather; also there is no ornamentation.

FASOLT's representative walks to the window and, looking at the magnificent view of the newly constructed city, begins in the tone used for pompous political oratory:

''Seldom in history have workers reaped the fruits of their toil. Usually a ruling class has taken it from them and placed its foot upon their necks. Both communism and democracy have tried to correct this condition and almost succeeded, but now we see before us the greatest injustice the world has ever known. You — you sovereigns — you hot-headed, irresponsible loafers, now fall heir to the fruit of all mankind's efforts for generations uncounted. The tyrannical bloodsuckers of the past have paid in the end — only their worthless blood, it is true — but it was all they had. You stand haughtily aloof and say that our citizens have paid too highly for their material civilization — that they have paid with their own souls and become tera-segments. Our bargain is kept; your city is finished. I wish there were more payment than your souls we could exact of you.''

Wotan, irritated, answers him, ''Judgment of history and men's souls is beyond your sphere. You are workers who have done a job. We are here to discuss your wage. Name it and let's be done with this damned build-up for bargaining.''

FASOLT's representative bristles as he turns. ''We have agreed on the only payment you are able to offer us. Our cities

41

WOTAN. You must be mad to ask for such a thing. Ask for some other wage. Freia you cannot have.

FASOLT. *(standing speechless in wrathful surprise)* What is this? Do you seek to betray a contract? Would you violate the contract that is written on your spear?

FAFNER. *(ironically)* My faithful brother! You fool. Don't you yet see the trick?

FASOLT. Son of light, and like light unstable. Hold on, and have a care. What you are is built on faithfulness to your treaties. There are limits to what you can do by might alone. You think you have greater wisdom than we have. Though we are pledged to peace, we can curse your wisdom, and let peaceful promises perish if you break warranted bond. A stupid giant tells you this. From him, you wise one, take fair warning.

WOTAN. How sly of you to pretend we were serious when plainly we were but jesting! The beautiful Goddess, light and bright — what use could she be to such as you.

FASOLT. Do you jeer at us? You of a proud and radiant race who foolishly want a tower of stone, and will trade for it a wondrous woman. We, stupid blockheads, toiling with toughened hands to win the wondrous woman. She, winning and sweet, should gladly go with us. But you now call your bond a jest.

FAFNER. Stop your childish chatter. There is nothing we can gain from Freia's charms. But the gods lose a lot if she is taken from them. Golden apples grow in her garden. No one but she can grasp the art of their culture. By eating them the gods gain eternal youth that time cannot ravish. If Freia were removed from among them, they would become weak and blighted and their beauty would pass. So, from them, Freia must be torn away!

have lost their vitality. We need new blood. You sovereigns have the blood of wild animals in your veins. With reluctance we have decided it must be mixed with ours.''

Disdainfully, Wotan answers, ''Mix it if you can with those who are old enough to have a free will. But you *cannot* take young women and children into the cities and make them into segments when they don't even know what is happening to them. Abduction and rape I will not permit.''

FASOLT's representative stands for a moment pretending to be speechless with amazement. ''What is this? The bargain calls for unmolested passage of all peoples between the wilds and the cities. The wording is clear and unmistakable. You, you who have risen to power by appealing to old romantic notions of honor, *you* of all men, can't hope to go back on your word and survive.''

FAFNER's representative says to FASOLT's, ''It was your nation that urged this treaty. We told you that these sovereigns were not above trying to maneuver out of a bargain. You see now that our warning was well-founded.''

FASOLT's representative turns to Wotan again and resumes his pompous tone, ''Wotan, leader of the sovereigns — of the men like gods — Wotan, a name that to every man on earth means steadfastness and honor, you knew full well our intention when the bargain was sealed. If you now think your reputation for honor so solid that you can stake it on taking advantage of a cunning play of words in a contract, words merely put in to save your romantic image, you will find that, although our desire is peace, we still remember how to fight.''

Wotan tells him, ''If it's only animal blood that you seek, there are still people on earth who have never been touched by the rise and fall of material civilizations. Nor do I seek to bring them under my influence. They are prolific and should have as much charm for your people as the wildsmaidens or even the most desirable of our sovereign beauties.''

With thinly veiled mockery, FASOLT's representative answers, ''We have listened to the story of *Men Like Gods*, to the tales of the pride and power of your men in combat and the beauty and tenderness of your women, until we are convinced that life without beauty is not life. We must have the daughters of the gods in our midst.''

FAFNER's representative explodes, ''Let's stop this childish chatter! This is no way to approach a conference table. If we are to start discussion now, let's drop the damned oratory and lay out

WOTAN. Loge lingers too long!

FASOLT. We are waiting for your word.

WOTAN. Ask some other wage.

FASOLT. No other. Freia alone.

FAFNER. You there, come with us. *(They press towards Freia.)*

FREIA. *(seeking to escape)* Help! Help me avoid these harsh ones. *(Donner and Froh enter hastily.)*

FROH. To me, Freia. *(He clasps her in his arms and speaks to Fafner.)* Stand back, you overbold one. Froh guards the goddess.

DONNER. *(placing himself before the two giants)* Fasolt and Fafner, don't you remember that you have felt my hammer blow before.

FAFNER. What's the meaning of this threat?

FASOLT. Why do you thrust in here? We are not looking for a fight. We want only what is due us.

DONNER. *(swinging his hammer)* I've given many giants their due. Come on! I'll give you what is due you, and give it in generous measure.

WOTAN. *(stretching out his spear between the disputants)* Hold back, you fierce one! All treaties are under protection of my spear. Put up your hammer. No force here.

the facts. We don't give a good god damn for any romantic notions of pride and beauty. Our races are dying and we must have new blood or perish. That is a simple matter. But there is no point in acting naive; we all know full well that we have still another purpose. We want to take the bloom from the cult of individual sovereignty — the cult of personal freedom, strength and beauty, that has made the sovereigns so damned productive. In three generations they have come from a few roving wild beings to a race of ever greater strength and vigor. We would like to appropriate some of their successful propaganda even while we are destroying them." He turns to Wotan and continues, "You knew it was becoming an idealogical battle and sought to bolster your position with a city equal to ours. We will also bolster our position by siphoning off your vitality and appropriating your propaganda in every way permitted by our treaty. And that's the whole of it."

Wotan turns to Fricka and says, "See if any word has come from Logi, will you?"

FASOLT's representative tries to talk as hard as FAFNER's, "Does the treaty become effective today as written?"

Wotan answers, "It was made subject to renegotiation before becoming effective."

FASOLT's representative continues his hard, defiant tone, "But only if other terms were mutually agreeable."

FAFNER's representative injects, "We have no other terms to propose. Apparently, neither have you."

Fricka has asked after Logi and also sent for Donner. Meeting Donner at the door, she brings him in. He wears a blue cloth military uniform. She introduces him by saying, "Logi is not here yet, but Donner should have a voice in this treaty."

Donner measures FAFNER's and FASOLT's representatives with his eyes and says, "It is not at a conference table that I talk. You have heard my words before and you know they are thunder."

FAFNER's representative turns to Wotan and asks, "What is the meaning of this threat?"

FASOLT's representative also turns to Wotan and adds, "We have come to review the treaty as agreed and we ask nothing but what is our due."

Donner injects, "I was reluctant once but I would now like nothing better than to give you your due in full measure."

Wotan speaks to all, "For that too I would gladly give my life but honor is more than life. What I have agreed to in treaty,

FREIA. Woe's me. Woe's me! Wotan forsakes me!

FRICKA. Is that your meaning, you merciless man?

WOTAN. *(turns away and sees Loge coming.)* Here is Loge! Are you hot in the haste to settle your badly-made bargain?

LOGE. *(has come up out of the valley in the background.)* What is this bargain for which I am blamed? Wasn't it you and the giants who bargained together? Over hill and hollow, I wander where my whim takes me. House and home hold no appeal for me. Donner and Froh are ones who want a fair dwelling. They want wives, so a house they must find. A bright abode, a stately hall, a spectacular fort — was also Wotan's wish. Well, a house and hall, a castle and court, a spectacular abode now pridefully stands awaiting. The towering walls I examined myself. Everything is firm. Fasolt and Fafner kept their part of the bargain. I have not been idle during all the construction. Whoever calls me a sluggard, he lies!

WOTAN. Artfully, you try to escape! Of all the gods, I alone have stood by you as a friend. Now speak, and speak clearly. When they who built the burg talked of Freia as payment, I consented only because you promised to find a way to ransom the glorious pledge.

LOGE. I agreed to give my full attention toward seeking a way to save Freia. That only did I promise. How could I possibly promise what I could not know — what substitute payment would be acceptable?

however unwisely, I will defend.''

Fricka breaks in, ''Can you stand quietly by with the cries of abducted women and children ringing in your ears and talk of honor?''

A guard opens the door and Logi enters. He is dressed in a business suit of the same type as the teras' representatives, but is conspicuously better groomed than they. He carries a briefcase and has the quick precise movements of an efficient man who has been hurrying. Wotan is obviously relieved at seeing him and expresses it in his intonation as he says, ''Here comes Logi.'' Then he speaks to Logi with a military air, ''More haste would have been commendable in coming to settle your sorry, badly made bargain.''

Before answering Wotan, Logi bows formally to the teras' representatives who return his bows. Then with poise he addresses himself to Wotan, ''What is this bargain for which I am blamed? I am but your attorney, your counselor, guarding you as best I can from the contractual snares in which your enemies would enmesh you. The decisions you make yourself. I am merely a vagabond with clean fingernails, a bystander in the affairs of teras, segments, and sovereigns. As a bystander I am disgusted frequently, amused often, sometimes delighted, but always free from faith or ties or ambitions. You sovereigns, drunk with the glory of your own achievements, just like the establishment fools, have sought a hall, a city, a physical monument that would proclaim to your own eyes and the eyes of others the grandeur of your achievements. Well, you have it now, a material grandeur unexcelled anywhere on the face of the earth. The workmanship is sound and every contractual obligation the teras have faithfully fulfilled. To assure this was my job. I have done it well.''

''Don't evade the point at issue,'' Wotan says, but he is not impatient. ''Your competence as a lawyer no one questions. Often I am warned to trust no more than your professional ability, but I, alone among the sovereigns, have stood as your friend, and sought your counsel as a man who is more than an attorney. It was only on your assurance that we would be able to renegotiate and do so without losing everyting the name sovereign stands for, that I agreed to the contract as originally written.''

Logi answers, ''I promised to seek for a substitute agreement that would be satisfactory to the teras. But I could not say what would be acceptable and what unacceptable to them, nor was I fool enough to make a positive promise.''

FRICKA. See, now, what a treacherous rogue you have trusted.

FROH. You are called Loge, but a better name for you is Liar.

DONNER. Accursed flame, I will put out your fire.

LOGE. You only turn on me in attempt to hide your own blundering.

(Donner threatens to strike Loge.)

WOTAN. *(stepping between them)* Let Loge alone. You know his way of doing things. His slowly given advice gains in worth if we only wait for it.

FAFNER. No more waiting. We want full payment, now.

FASOLT. We have done with waiting.

WOTAN. *(to Loge)* Speak up, strategist. What have you discovered in your travels here and there?

LOGE. You give no gratitude for my efforts. I have gone to the ends of the earth seeking a substitute for Freia that the giants would consider just. I searched in vain. In all the world I found nothing that men value above a woman's wonderous worth.

(All show surprise and disappointment.)

Wherever I found life flowing and ebbing, in the water, on the earth, and in the air, everywhere I asked what would a man value higher than a woman's love. But everywhere my inquiry was met with laughter. In the water, on the earth, and in the air, everywhere love is the thing on which all place greatest value. And yet I did meet one who had forsworn love for ruddy gold. The Rhine-maidens had a sorrowful tale for me. The Nibelung, Night-Alberich, sought favor from the Rhine-maidens and their favors they refused him. In his raging revenge, he took from them their Rhinegold. He now values the worth of the stolen Rhinegold as greater than a woman's love. The Rhine-maidens grieve greatly over their loss. It is to you, Wotan, they look as one to deal with the robber. They want the Rhinegold returned to its rightful place and there for it to remain forever. I swore to bring their plea to you. Now, faithful to my word, I have laid their plea before you.

"See, now, the sort of treacherous rogue you have trusted," Fricka burst in.

"Legality has always been known as a polite name for lies," Donner adds. "If I had my way we would dispense with treaties and speak only with force." He turns and speaks to Logi with open dislike, "Shall I give you a language lesson?"

As if stepping between them Wotan says, "Hold your violence for our enemies. Logi has the training of a lawyer and we have to be patient with his attention to the precision of phraseology. When he gets around to the substance of things his judgment is sound."

FAFNER's representative says, "If there is going to be substance to this conversation, then get on with it."

"Yes," FASOLT's adds, "propaganda made of clever words is food only for the masses. In the privacy of a closed session conference room you cannot meet obligations with mere words."

"Let's hear it, Logi," Wotan says. "You have been away for many months. What have you discovered? I'm looking to you for something good. Don't fail me."

"Still only reproach," Logi begins. "I have no faith, but I continue trying to save you, though why I don't know. Yet these months, too, I have been at the old task. I have roamed among all people to the ends of the earth and studied carefully their motivating desires and aspirations. The two prime movers in the drama of human destiny are love, born of the sexual heritage, and the will to power, born of the more primitive asexual organic being. By channelling both into a world of make believe, where they find a vicarious outlet in dreams on a television screen, the teras gained control of the world and reduced its people to something less than their organic heritage. Their so-called 'civilization' crystallized into its recognizable character when the power of mass opinion was admittedly made supreme, when politics became nothing but a TV program, and politicians became nothing but script writers and actors. The teras have reached a dead end. The power of public opinion feeds on itself and destroys its own vitality. This fact was acknowledged by the whimsical designer of the award for the best television program each year — the Ring in the form of a Uroborus, a snake swallowing its own tail. With the example of the teras still before us, it would be thought that no one would again seek power by courting capricious public opinion."

"We don't need one of your damned lectures on history," FAFNER's representative interrupts.

WOTAN. Are you insensitive enough not to see that, in my own plight, I can be of no help to others?

FASOLT. *(who has been listening attentively — to Fafner)* I don't like to see the Nibelung have control of the Rhinegold. He has already done us much harm, and we have never been able to deal with him.

"You are right," Logi answers him. "It's too late for you to benefit by it. But there still may be some hope for Wotan. He's not yet fully committed and *he's* not a hopeless fool."

He turns back to Wotan, "Fools unwittingly stumble into the Ring's trap but to wield the power of the Ring the conscious master must forswear love, love of woman and love of basic creation. No whole man will forego love, but the world — even the wilds — has many men with the souls of dwarfs. Alber even now is following the paths taken by the teras in their early formation. He has acquired title to land by trinkets, as the Americans once did from the Indians, and has made work contracts that are as harmless looking and as fiendish as their prototypes of the twentieth century. Already his Ring is being fashioned as it has been in the past — the natural wealth of the wilds is being transformed into manufactured articles. These made into status symbols produce the Ring in its original and crudest form. He who controls and manipulates their lure without scruple holds the power of the world."

Logi pauses, and Wotan by a gesture urges him to go on. He continues, "Many of the wildsmaidens are torn between their desire for baubles and their sorrow at seeing their once laughing lovers turned into wage slaves, into organizational segments who are less than men. They bewail their fate and, now that it seems too late for them to help themselves, they remember your admonition. They have asked me to bring you their cry for aid. For what good it will do, I have brought it."

"What good indeed! I ask from them steadfastness to the ideals of Freia and Froh* and instead they sell themselves out, and at the moment of my own great need ask me for help."

FASOLT's representative has been listening attentively and now speaks to FAFNER's. "Alber, the Nibelung — as you well know — has always been our worst enemy. It was he, an outcast from one of *your* cities who started the raids on *our* cities and led to Donner's bringing his bomber force into Wotan's camp. It was our delight in Wotan's fight with Alber that prompted our program *Men Like Gods*.

---

*Freia and Froh: The heroine and hero of the program "Men Like Gods." They represent the sovereign ideals of woman and man.

FAFNER. Now with the Rhinegold, the Nibelung will be an even greater annoyance. Listen Loge, tell us the full truth. What great use can the dwarf make of the Rhinegold that makes it so desirable to him?

LOGE. In the possession of the Rhine-maidens it is something good only to bring them joy. But when a Ring is made from it, it brings its holder power over the whole world.

WOTAN. I have heard many rumors of the Rhinegold, how it gives wealth and might to its holder when it is made into a ring.

FRICKA. Does the ring made from the Rhinegold also hold a value for women?

LOGE. A wife could hold her husband firmly if she had the ring that the slaving dwarfs are fashioning from the radiant mass.

FRICKA. *(coaxingly to Wotan)* Couldn't my husband get this for me?

WOTAN. I think the smart thing would be for me to hold the ring. But tell me, Loge, could I learn to fashion the treasure?

LOGE. The process works like magic, but none can know it without first forswearing love.

FAFNER's representative agrees, "He will still be a worse enemy than Wotan if he gains enough power. Wotan has agreed not to bomb our cities. The agreement between Wotan and us to use, not just no atomic weapons, but no explosive weapons of any kind in the wildslands works to Alber's gain. He is already building cities in the wildsland composed of fresh vital people and building them under the protection of our treaties. Someway he must be stopped." He turns to Logi and asks, "Does Alber yet have any real power?"

Logi answers carefully, "He is doing a sound business in trade and transportation, fish to the interior, corn and grain to the coast, fur and skins from the hunters, lumber to the villagers. He has soundly operated factories. He has been fair beyond belief to everyone and has sweetened his bargains with gifts stolen over the years from the cities — not to mention payment you have made to him for abducted wildsmaidens. He has title to all lands and work contracts throughout all Nibelung. He has brought back the idea of rule by public voting, the secret ballot, from the twentieth century. With this to make his real power invisible he is now beginning to tighten his control."

Wotan shows a new interest and says, "I have heard something of the maneuvers by which the teras originally gained their power over the people — manufactured articles held constantly before their eyes like a hypnotic light, while their freedom was taken from them inch by inch, through public ballots they themselves cast."

Fricka asks softly of Logi, "Did not the women have things very good under that system? Didn't they have a voice in how things were run — equal votes and equal rights in all things?"

He answers, "Not only to vote and control men's power did women have the privilege; it was mostly to gain value in the eyes of their women that men accepted the system."

Fricka turns to Wotan and asks, "Would it not be well for you to hold this power over people and turn it to worthy use?"

He has been following his own train of thought along the same line and continues it by saying, "Although the system was used for leading fools to greater folly, there will always be many fools in the world. My appeals to reason and honor have not always been successful. Perhaps there are some who could be swayed better by this cunning device." He turns to Logi and asks, "Do you think I could learn to handle it?"

"Anyone can learn if power, and power only, is his goal," Logi answers. "But remember this: The one who handles it

(Wotan turns away discouraged.)
That doesn't appeal to you. Well too late you are, too. Alberich did not hesitate. Promptly he conquered the potent spell, and effectively fashioned the ring.

DONNER. We will all fall under his power, if the ring is not taken from him.

WOTAN. That ring I must capture.

FROH. Lightly now, without forswearing love, you would win it.

LOGE. Just so, without guile, as in children's games!

WOTAN. Then tell us how.

LOGE. By theft! What the thief stole, steal from the thief! Could anything be easier. But Alberich fights with clever weapons. Shrewd and scheming your strategy will need to be if you are going to outdo this robber. And restore the Rhinegold to the Rhine-maidens, as they plead with you to do.

WOTAN. To the Rhine-maidens? What would I gain by that?

FRICKA. Nothing of that billow-born brood do I want to hear. For much to my woe, they have lured many a man to their caves.

(Wotan stands silently struggling with himself, while the other gods all look expectantly toward him. Meanwhile Fafner has consulted aside with Fasolt.)

FAFNER. *(to Fasolt)* The Rhinegold could be worth much more to us than Freia. Eternal youth, too, could be ours if we mastered the Rhinegold's full power. *(Fasolt's gestures indicate that he is being convinced against his will. Fafner and Fasolt approach Wotan again.)* Hear, Wotan. Our hasty new terms. We will restore Freia to you, and accept a lesser payment. We stupid giants will settle for the Rhinegold that the Nibelung now holds.

successfully must be truly ruthless. He cannot merely be oblivious to the physical pain and death he causes, as a warrior must be when he meets his enemy. He must be ruthless in what he does to men's souls, to their self-respect, and to their honor. He can have no compassion and no love, neither for man, nor for woman, nor for anything hallowed by all the aeons of creation."

Wotan turns away in annoyance. Logi comments, "That does not suit you, huh? Alber has no such scruples. He has fashioned the prototype of the same Ring that in the cities now continues only as hypnotic entertainment."

Donner has become disturbed by what is being said and addresses Wotan, "We will all fall to the power of that dwarf if the treaty that protects the wildslands from explosive weapons is not changed so I can deal with him."

Wotan has no hesitation in answering, "No. The Ring I must take from Alber but not in that way."

"Just so: Without guile, everything done by *verbal* rules, like in children's games," ridicules Logi.

"Then tell us how," Wotan demands.

"By stealth!" Logi answers him quickly. "What the thief stole you must steal from the thief. What could be more fitting and effective? But Alber is no fool. You are going to have to do some smart scheming if you get from him the title to the land that has been vested in the State of Nibelung. You will also have to get the contracts that his industries and unions have worked up, if you are going to return a free land, and free men instead of slaves, as lovers, to the wildsmaidens."

"To the wildsmaidens!" Wotan explodes. "Tear up the contracts and restore the land to wild domain? By that I would gain nothing."

"I'm tired of hearing of the unspoiled beauty of the wildsmaidens," Fricka says indignantly. "There is never a regiment in Godsland that can muster full strength because its warriors are out with them in some cave in the forest or by the sea."

For a long time Wotan stands silently struggling with himself. The other sovereigns gaze at him a little surprised that he would pause to consider a dishonorable course. FAFNER's representative meanwhile has been consulting aside with FASOLT's. In the silence FAFNER's representative is heard saying, "We could concede Wotan's point of not taking maidens and children into the cities if we could get the toe-hold Alber has gained toward building cities in the wilds. We would be starting with new blood

WOTAN. You must be mad! How can I give you in payment something that is not yet in my possession.

FAFNER. Hard labor went into the construction of yonder towers. It would be easy for you, with fraud-aided force, to capture and hold the Nibelung.

WOTAN. Why should I make war on the Nibelung — fight your foe for you? You have become insolent and greedy because I'm in debt to you.

FASOLT. *(suddenly seizes Freia and drags her to one side with Fafner.)* Come here, maiden! We claim you as ours! We'll hold you as pledge until the ransom is paid.

(Freia cries loudly. All the gods look on in the greatest perturbation.)

FAFNER. Far from among you, we'll take and hold her. Until evening — remember it well — we'll hold her as pledge. Then we will return. If the Rhinegold is not waiting for us —

FASOLT. It is the end of your opportunity. Freia will be the forfeit. She will be ours forever.

FREIA. Sisters! Brothers! Save me. Help!

(She is dragged along by the hastily retreating giants. The troubled gods hear her screams dying away in the distance.)

FROH. Let's go after them!

and we could keep it vital." Then they draw further aside and talk together unheard. FASOLT's representative's gestures indicate that he is being convinced against his will.

FAFNER's representative now speaks as they both approach Wotan, "Hear, Wotan. We offer substitute terms. We will set up safeguards, under your own control, to insure that no minors will be taken into our cities without full consent of their parents or guardians. In return you will place the man we pick for a joint administrator in the contractual position now held by Alber."

"You are mad, both of you," Wotan tells them. "How can I give you what I do not, myself, possess?"

FAFNER's representative answers calmly, "You have great influence and many faithful followers in all the wilds, including the lands of the Nibelung. It would be easy for you to move in on Alber. He is becoming vulnerable, now that he is getting over ambitious and beginning to drive too hard."

Wotan may simply be thinking aloud but his words are spoken in answer to the proposal, "I have fought to make men free throughout the world. And now that I have dealt with you by treaties you think of me as one of your kind, and have the insolence to propose that I seize a people in bondage and deliver them over to you with the bonds intact."

FASOLT's representative ostentatiously rises to conclude the conference, "As you will. We have free passage in all the wildsland under your protection. We will talk of restrictions elsewhere in return for a free hand in Nibelung."

Fricka looks at Wotan and asks, "To what depths of ignominy have the sovereigns sunk?"

FAFNER's representative summarizes, "The treaty as written becomes effective today. In six months we will meet with you again. If you deliver to us then full control in Nibelung and leave the cold steel weapon's clause intact, we will respect absolutely the boundaries of Godsland; you will respect absolutely the old boundaries of FAFNER and FASOLT, and the rest of the wildslands will continue the status they had before today's treaty."

FASOLT's representative adds, "That offer is our last. If the terms are not met in full at the time stated, there will be no further negotiations and today's treaty will stand indefinitely, perhaps forever."

The representatives leave with a display of official firmness and dramatic finality. When the door has been closed behind them, Fricka turns on Wotan, "Do you not hear the screams of our sisters

DONNER. Let the heavens fall!

LOGE. *(watching the giants)* Stumbling over the stones, they are going down the valley. They are going through the ford and crossing the Rhine. They stumble and fall and Freia, carried on their backs, takes a beating with every stumble. All through the Rhine valley they reel. They won't stop to rest until they reach the Riesenhelm's boundary. *(He turns and looks at the gods.)* What does Wotan dream that darkens his face so much? What ails, the high, happy gods?

(A pale mist, gradually increasing in density, fills the stage. Seen through it the gods seem to take on an aged and haggard appearance. All stand in dismay looking at Wotan, whose eyes are fixed broodingly on the ground.)

LOGE. Does the mist mock me? Does it trick me to have dark dreams? How fast your fair faces seem to be fading. The bloom is going from your cheeks, and the sparkle from your eyes. Courage Froh, day has just begun. From your relaxed hand, Donner, the hammer is slipping. And what distresses Fricka? Is she disturbed that Wotan's hair, growing grey, makes him look gloomy and old?

FRICKA. Woe's me. Woe's me. What does it all mean.

DONNER. My hand sinks down.

FROH. My heart stands still.

LOGE. I have it! I'll tell you what has happened. You haven't eaten of Freia's fruit today. The golden apples from her garden preserved you from dwindling with age. You always ate of them every day. The garden's keeper is now a captive, and the fruit rots on the branches. Soon the spoiled fruit will fall and be gone. My problem is milder. Freia has always given me but half as much as she has given to you more favored ones. You all depended on Freia's apples. Of this the giants were well aware. They plotted against your very lives. Without the apples, the gods will grow old and grim, gray and gruesome, and, scoffed at by all the world, they will waste and pass away.

and daughters in your ears?'' Wotan is trying to think and pays her no attention.

Donner addresses Wotan formally, ''Any weight my words had in our present plight I would now recall. Let us give them our answer from the heavens.''

Without answering, Wotan sinks dejectedly into a chair while Donner and Fricka watch him in silent inquiry. Logi, at the window watching the teras' planes take off, voices his own thoughts for all to hear, ''We must consider what course the teras will take during the next six months. They might keep down abduction incidents to win confidence in the wilds. Or they might start wild rioting to bring pressure on Wotan to meet their terms. They could each try to play a separate game but I think they fear each other too much for that. No matter what they do, their propaganda mills will be in full production every hour of every day.''

He turns and looks at the sovereigns. He looks at them long and thoughtfully then says, ''How darkly dreams the great Wotan! What ails the high, once happy sovereigns — the men like gods?''

The fire, that has been burning brightly on the hearth, dies to a feeble flame. The sun has moved until it no longer reflects through the windows and gloom prevails in the room. All stand in dismay and apprehension regarding Wotan, whose eyes are fixed broodingly on the table.

Logi continues, ''Does the light of the room mock me —giving substance to a dream I would not dream? The youth, the joy, the strength and beauty seem to be fading from your faces and the sparkle and brightness from your eyes. Courage Froh! A smile of tender love and confidence Freia! Why so dejected, Donner, do you not command the greatest air force on earth? And look at Fricka. Does such a scowl become the first lady of all sovereigns? And Wotan, whose youth and strength and power are legend throughout the world, looks today like a tired old man.''

Fricka admits. ''I have never felt less like the first lady of all sovereigns than I do at this moment.''

Donner adds, ''And I, who have power to destroy the world, cannot keep my head from falling on my chest.''

''You speak to others of strength through joy,'' Logi says, ''but you have had no taste of freedom's food today. You live and rule by joy in freedom, love, and beauty. But today you have sat at the table with the teras and had only such rations as they give to their segments. I do not suffer so much as you. Being an observer, I live less by joy than by mere interest and amusement.

FRICKA. Wotan, you lost man. See what your laughing lightness has brought us — scoff and scorn for us all.

WOTAN. *(starting up with sudden resolution)* Up! Loge. Come with me. Downward, to the home of the Nibelungs, we'll go and take the Rhinegold.

LOGE. It was then not in vain that the Rhine-maidens turned to you for help.

WOTAN. Fool, be silent. It is Freia's ransom that we are going for.

LOGE. Gladly I'll go wherever you want. Shall we dive through the depths of the Rhine?

WOTAN. Not through the Rhine.

LOGE. Then let us swing through this smoky chasm. Together, come, slip through with me.

(He goes first and disappears at the side down a crevice from which immediately a sulphurous vapor rises.)

WOTAN. You others wait here till evening. The ransom I'll get and we'll regain our youth.

(He descends after Loge in the chasm. The sulphurous vapor which rises from it spreads over the whole stage and quickly fills it with thick clouds, concealing the rest of the characters.)

DONNER. Fare you well, Wotan!

FROH. Good luck. Good luck.

FRICKA. Come back soon to your sorrowing wife.

(The sulphurous vapor thickens to a black cloud, which rises upwards from below. This then changes to a firm, gloomy, rocky cavern which keeps rising, so that the stage seems to sink deeper and deeper into the earth.)

But you sovereigns are what you are because the prime movers of life have flowed in your beings as freely as a mountain stream. They have not been damned up and diverted to turn the wheels of industry, nor been made to squeeze under tension through the intricate machinations of power politics. You have loved freely and fought freely, lived freely and died freely. And by the beauty of your integrity, your spontaneity, and your truth you have ruled. But today the teras have taken your youth and beauty. Tomorrow they will take your power. This you know must be true. Their propaganda soon seeps into the wilds." They have all settled down at the table and Logi now joins them.

Fricka addresses Wotan, anxiously, "Wotan! Do you hear Logi? For once he speaks truth. See what your laughing lightness has brought the sovereigns — scoff and scorn for all!"

Wotan, coming to a sudden resolve, stands up. "Up, Logi, and come with me! If such control as Alber holds, is a thing that can be passed from hand to hand, my hand shall hold it."

Logi rises, "Then it was not in vain that the wildsmaidens sent appeal to you in their distress?"

"Don't talk like a fool. We can keep nothing free but the Godsland."

Logi shrugs, "No more? Well how do you propose to go about this? By arousing your followers in the wilds?"

Wotan answers, "Not now. Much as I dislike it, we'll try it your way — the devious route of legality."

Logi confirms the plan, "Then we'll seek the confidence of Alber's opposition. We'll work our way into control under cover and by duplicity, just as he has done." He fills his briefcase and leads the way through the door in whimsical amusement.

Wotan turns before going through the door and says, "See that no one does or says *anything* that can be turned to propaganda. The Godsland will again be free, and we who have lost this battle may yet win the war."

THIRD SCENE

From various points in the distance ruddy lights gleam out. An increasing clamor, as of smiths at work, is heard from all sides. The clang of anvils dies away. A vast subterranean cavern becomes visible which seems to open into narrower passages on all sides. Alberich enters, dragging the shrieking Mime by the ear from a passage at one side.)

ALBERICH. Hehe! Hehe! Come here! Come here! Scheming dwarf. I'll pinch your ear good if you don't at once weld me the special work I have shown you.

MIME. *(howling)* Ohe! Ohe! Oh! Oh! Let me alone. Heeding your command, I have labored hard, and it is done. Take your fingernails out of my ear.

ALBERICH. Then why this delay? Let me have it.

MIME. I feared that something might be lacking.

ALBERICH. What is left to finish?

MIME. *(hesitating)* Here — and there —

ALBERICH. How "here and there"? Hand me your work.

(He threatens to sieze Mime again by the ear. Mime, in terror, lets fall a piece of metal work that he has held concealed. Alberich hastily picks it up and examines it.)

ALBERICH. See, you deceiver. It is all finished. It is done as I planned. You sought to deceive me and save the wonderful work for yourself. Without my planning you could have done nothing alone. I know your scheming thoughts. *(He sets the finished work on his head as a "Tarnhelm.")* This helm fits the head. Now will it do what it ought? — "Night obscure me, make me invisible." *(He vanishes, and a column of smoke takes his place.)* Brother, do you see me?

III

A spacious executive office furnished in exaggerated elegance can now be seen. There is a luxurious reception alcove, an enormous, highly polished conference table, and a large executive desk. The backwall has heavy drapes, controlled by push buttons, which when opened reveal a life-size television screen.

Alber, wearing slightly flashy business dress, enters, banging doors and throwing his coat at the desk, knocking a book, ashtrays, and knick-knacks clattering to the floor. He calls loudly, "Mime! Mime! Come here! Come here!" and through the open door of the adjoining office Mime enters at once. Mime's appearance is similar to that of Alber but his mannerisms are furtive and lacking in vitality.

Alber grabs him by the coat and slaps him on both sides of the face as he says, "God damn you and your slippery tricks! I need your slimy skill at politics but don't try a double cross on me. Nobody double-crosses Alber and lives — nobody!"

"What's the matter, Alber? What are you talking about? I haven't double-crossed you. Everything is going like clockwork. We've already got the smoothest, best oiled, political machine that ever existed."

"But who's controlling it? Who's controlling it? I just had to liquidate a real smart precinct boss who got too damned cocky. I hated to do it. I really liked the god damned bastard. He was a smart manipulator. But he told me — me, Alber — that he took his orders from Mime."

"They all know I'm not the boss, but you know there are a lot left who would balk if they knew you called the shots."

"We've got to be able to handle these balkers now. We've got to get moving."

"There are still some..." Mime tries to protest.

Alber cuts him short, "We threw that north-end election to my man last week by a big majority. And look at that landslide vote last month in the west after that long TV build-up. That was the west where we're weakest. With enough propaganda fed to them the damn fools would vote to have their own stupid heads chopped off. My control is tight now and your story that you still need to set up dummy opposition to me, something for people to

MIME. *(gazing about in astonishment)* Where are you? I see no one.

ALBERICH. *(voice)* Then feel me instead, you faithless scamp, take this for your thievish tricks!

MIME. *(writhes and screams from blows which are heard to fall on him from an invisible source.)*

ALBERICH. *(invisible, laughing)* I thank you, dumbskull. Your work was well performed. Hoho! Hoho! Nibelung elves will now all kneel to Alberich! Alberich will wander everywhere carefully watching. The period of rest is gone forever. You must serve him whom none can see. When you least of all expect him, he will be right by you. You will be his slaves forever. Hoho! Hoho! Hear him. He's near you. The ruler of the Nibelungs!

(The column of smoke disappears towards the back. Alberich's scolding voice is heard retreating in the distance. Howls and cries come from the distance. Mime has huddled up in pain. His groans and whimpers are heard by Wotan and Loge who descend from a cleft above.)

LOGE. Nibelhelm's here. What glare is that that comes from yonder smoke column?

hang their faith on, is beginning to sound suspicious. And another thing! Some of the opposition looks too god-damned real to suit me. You start playing down personalities more. Understand! You play up economics, play up high interest rates, play up minority issues, play up unemployment. Play up labor and industry conflicts. Give the dopes some harmless problems to think about. Get some voter's petitions circulating. Let them forget who's running things. You concentrate on the old tried and true bullshit, that old bullshit that the voters are the boss. You bear down on that. It has *always* worked. Mr. Average Citizen is running things — MR. AVERAGE CITIZEN — the invisible man. And *I* am Mr. Average Citizen. I'm just a face in the crowd. You can't see me.''

"O.K. Alber. O.K. You're the boss and I don't see you.''

''But don't forget that you can feel me. My boys are anxious to work you over. They hate your slimy guts. And I could enjoy a little perverted entertainment myself — with you as the victim.'' Alber grabs Mime's coat, twists it against his throat, and grins to show the pleasure full strangulation would give him.

"Take it easy Alber. I can still give you a lot of help.''

Alber laughs but keeps choking, ''Yeah. Maybe you can. But you'd damned well better hope you can keep it up.'' He relaxes and becomes expansive. ''You're a snivelling bastard. But you're not so bad at politics. I've got a pretty good machine. All I've got to do is stay invisible and I can tighten down now. These Nibelungs are a dumb god-damned bunch of romantic idealists. But their days of lolling on the beach or playing peek-a-boo with their little wildsmaidens among the trees are over. They're going to work, work, work! They are going to work until they're too damn tired to think of rioting.'' He becomes thoughtful, then jerks himself together with sudden resolution and says, ''Hand me my coat there. I'm going out and let a few of my favorite enemies lick their master's boots.''

Mime helps him on with his coat and he goes out. When he is gone Mime clenches his fists and grinds his teeth at the door through which Alber left.

Logi and Wotan are shown in by a secretary through another door just in time to see Mime's gesture. He turns, sees them and tries to camouflage his gesture by taking his head in his hands as if suffering from a painful headache.

Pretending to be taken in by the camouflage, Logi says, ''We have seen the work you have been doing and are not surprised to find you tired.''

WOTAN. Who groans so loudly? Who's this that lies on the ground?

LOGE. *(bending down over Mime)* Why all this whimpering and whining?

MIME. Ohe! Ohe! Oh! Oh!

LOGE. Hey, Mime, happy dwarf. Who beats and bullies you like this?

MIME. Leave me in peace, please.

LOGE. Yes, without question. And still more. Listen. Help, I offer you, Mime.

MIME. *(partially rising)* What help is there for me? My brother can force me to do as he says. I am hopelessly his slave.

LOGE. But, Mime, what brought him the power to command?

MIME. With evil methods, Alberich turned the Rhinegold into a ruddy ring that, through a spell of magic, masters our spirits. With this he moves the night-loving Nibelung race to serve him. Once at our anvils we made only ornaments to please our wives, or worked from the ore nice little Nibelung toys. With light enjoyment, we once laughed while we worked. Now Alberich compels us to go creeping into the caverns and work only for him. Using the ring, he determines where unknown splendor is spread in the earth. Then we all trace it down, dig it, extract the metal and melt it into bars. With no peace or pause, we must all heap up the hoard for him.

Mime makes an affected gesture of suffering and says, "Your pardon, gentlemen — my head is splitting."

Wotan comments, "You groan like a thing whipped and defeated."

Logi adds, "There is more than weariness in your sighing."

Mime makes another exaggerated gesture of shaking a headache.

"Relax, Mime," Logi soothes. "You were once a happy dwarf. Who has taken all the old joy out of your life?"

"Have you come only to make jokes about my sufferings?"

Logi tells him, "Our coming may well remove your suffering's real cause."

"I seem beyond help. I always end up a stooge and work horse for some gore-happy numbskull like Alber."

Logi tries to open real conversation. "How does it happen this time? You were number two boy in FAFNER before they exiled you. Alber was nowhere near your class when you were both in FAFNER's political setup. He was little more than a racket boss. How come he's number one and you're number two here?"

Mime responds to Logi's tone. "Alber is a political genius. It's that simple. And his racket boss background was the best possible training for practical politics. Political control is simply a matter of grabbing wealth by taxation, dangling it before all eyes as something easy to get without risking your neck, then, in the political scramble, playing one man's ideals against another 'for the common good.' The political principal is simple. But it takes someone like Alber, a cheap crook with no love for anybody or anything to use it effectively. I'm a politician by education. A politician just by education. I'm too damned academic. Alber is a born politician."

When he pauses, Logi and Wotan give him a chance to go on and he takes it. "The common good," he says, "is, of course, just a translation that makes palatable to people with ideals the basic proposition of all successful politicians: Ideals have one common denominator — power. Whoever reduces them to this common denominator can use opposing ideals for a single purpose — any purpose. That purpose can be attractively named for public consumption or completely obscured. This I well understand. I was educated as a child for my place in FAFNER. My downfall there was that I got attracted to a faction. Here my weakness was that I was beginning to enjoy being a free man. I might even have become a sovereign. I sometimes wonder if I

LOGE. Just now, then, an idler roused himself to correct your laziness?

MIME. I started off badly. And my lot is the hardest. I had to forge the helmet he uses. He gave me exact instructions how to do it. I could see the wondrous might that came from the helmet that I made from steel. I badly wanted it for myself. With its power, I could be free from enslavement to Alberich and maybe — yes, maybe — I might become master over the master ruler, himself. If I could steal from him the ring, then his slave would thereafter command his master.

LOGE. And, why, you schemer, did your plan not work?

MIME. Ah! Although I did the work, the magic I was unable to fully grasp. From him who robbed me of my own work, I just now learned — too late — how to use my work's power. While from my sight he vanished, my back now shows welts from his beating. Because of my own foolishness, this was my thanks.

(He rubs his back, howling. The gods laugh.)

LOGE. You can see that our task will call for skill.

WOTAN. To accomplish this task, I rely on your skill.

didn't even join Alber with the idea that I might throw some weight in the cause of freedom. Of course I'm no damn romantic like you guys. I planned to get a few good things for myself.''

When he pauses this time Logi comments, ''But dividing your efforts between the cause of freedom, the cause of Mime, and the cause of Alber leaves you little time for idle enjoyment, huh?''

Mime affectedly places his hands on his head and sighs dramatically, ''Ah. I don't know how I stand it! The demands of a high administrative office never let up. I envy the laborers, the dock workers, even the miners. Alber drives from sheer love of driving; the pace is frantic. I have worked up a political machine in the Nibelung section of the wildslands almost equal to those in the tightly controlled nations before the big war. And I have done it in a few years. I was going along pretty well on my own in the east section. I had a solid start toward becoming a power to be reckoned with. Then Alber began moving in on my territory. I couldn't whip him so I joined him. I thought I might get control from the inside. But he pushed so damned hard he upset all my schemes before I could work them out. I might have been top man and thrown some weight for freedom. And now I'm simply his number one stooge.''

''It is truly amazing,'' Logi says, ''that he can beat a smart fellow like you at your own game, when you have so much the better background.''

''Yes,'' Mime goes on willingly. ''For what it's worth I suppose I know mass psychology, political strategy, and propaganda better than any man alive. And I have the actual experience. I have both the ideas and the know-how, but he has true genius. I work up a popular movement that the public thinks is democratic, while of course it is controlled by my own men, and he always knows just where and how much to threaten and promise in order to take control. He gets full control of the action without ever showing his hand. It's not only the stupid public that doesn't know where the power is and how to fight it. Even I get lost trying to follow the action. I'm never sure of my place nor my life from one day to the next.''

Logi addresses Wotan in a normal voice, intending for Mime to hear, ''I've known Mime since we were children. He has his weak points but you can depend absolutely on his political appraisals. This job is going to call for real skill.''

Wotan answers, ''You've lived with the teras. You know this game and how to handle tricky forces.''

MIME. *(struck by the laughter of the gods, observes them more attentively.)* Who are you, strangers, that you question me so freely?

LOGE. Friends to you. From their oppression, we would like to free all the Nibelung folk.

MIME. *(shrinking back in fear because he hears Alberich coming.)* Look out, Alberich is coming.

WOTAN. We'll wait for him here.

(Wotan sits down on a stone. Loge waits by his side. Alberich, who has taken the Tarnhelm from his head and hung it on his girdle, is brandishing his whip as he drives from the caves a crowd of Nibelungs. They are laden with gold and silver treasure and he pushes them to pile it all in a large heap.)

ALBERICH. Hither! Thither! Hehe! Hoho! You lazy herd! There in heaps pile up the hoard. You there, get up! Move on, move on. You indolent pack, stack up the ingots. Do you need my special urging? Well, move on then. *(He suddenly sees Wotan and Loge.)* Hey, who are these intruders. Mime, come here! What are you doing talking with this pair? Get back to your pickaxe and pincers.

(With his whip he drives MIme into the crowd of Nibelungs.)

ALBERICH. Hey! Off to your labors! And be quick about it. Hurry back below. Shovel the gold from the new found shafts. Whoever fails to work with a will gets my whip. If any are idle, Mime will answer for them, and my whip will ask the questions. I can see everything without being seen. No one knows this better than Mime. Are you still here? Get going!

(He pulls the ring from his finger, kisses it, and stretches it out with a commanding gesture.) Tremble in terror, fallen race, you will obey him who holds the ring.

Mime wants to come to the point, "You sent word that what you plan to do here would be to my interest."

Logi says, "Any boss but Alber will be an improvement for the people of Nibelung. Also any boss but Alber can be only an improvement for you."

Mime hears something and cautions, "Wait. Watch your speech. Alber is coming."

"We'll sit back here and observe," Wotan says. He and Logi settle in deep comfortable seats in an alcove where they are not readily seen from the rest of the office. Alber comes in with five of his strong-arm men and three minor officials to be given a lesson in obedience to orders. Their arms are hand-cuffed behind them. Two of his plain clothes thugs hold, while a third delivers heavy body blows to one official. Then Alber steps up and slaps him a few times across the face to attract his attention.

"Stand up and listen," Alber says. "You'll learn something of production methods. A plant superintendent has only one job — production. If his factory doesn't produce he's nothing, nothing — zero — kaput. I told you to give me results and I'd make you a big man. There's only one way to manage. I thought you *knew* it. Well I'm going to give you *one* lesson. Just *one*."

He suddenly sees Wotan and Logi, turns and violently addresses Mime, "What the god-damned-hell? Who are they? What are they doing here? Why didn't you say something?" He grabs Mime by the coat, then realizing who the guests are, he shoves Mime aside and faces them. "The high and noble gods! What! Have you come to take a course in administration from the master? Then observe."

He turns back and gives a nod to his thugs who brutally beat up the man they are holding. As he falls, they kick him into the corner. Meanwhile Alber continues to Wotan, "See. My words are actions. That was my memo to this plant superintendent telling him to increase production. If he gets another memo it will simply say, 'Too damned bad you didn't.' But he'll never read it."

He turns to the other two officials and nods to his thugs who release them. "Now you guys are new and I'd like to be nice to you. When my boys — my boys, not Mime's boys — bring you word to do something you do it and you don't ask why. There are five men on the committee tomorrow. One will go our way because he's just a good citizen with the public interest at heart. And you two will vote as you were told and carry the committee. I'm grooming you for big things if you show you can learn fast.

71

(With howls and shrieks, the Nibelungs — Mime among them — separate and slip into crevices on all sides and go down the shafts again.)

ALBERICH. *(looks long and distrustfully at Wotan and Loge.)* What do you want here?

WOTAN. Strange news has come to us of wonders worked by Alberich in Nibelhelm's night-bound land. To see these marvels we come here as your guests.

ALBERICH. Nothing prompts you but envy, I know. That is why you are here as my guests.

LOGE. Do you not know me, miserable dwarf. In your cold freezing lair, where would you find light and warmth if I had not been there. What would be the use of your hammer if I had not heated the forge? I am your kinsman, and once was a friend. I think you would do well to show more thanks.

ALBERICH. You have now joined up with the light-born people. If you are as false a friend to them as you were to me, that's good. Then, with you in their midst, I have nothing to fear from them.

LOGE. There is no need for all this distrust.

ALBERICH. I trust your falseness, not your truth. But I'm now safe. I dare all with no need for caution.

LOGE. Power has certainly boosted your spirit. Your force is becoming grimly great.

ALBERICH. You can see the hoard that my controlled people have heaped up for me.

You'll need prestige. So a couple of the boys will show you over to some apartments I've outfitted for you. You'll find out that I can be a damned nice guy to good public spirited citizens who know how to cooperate.'' He studies them intently before saying a last word threatingly and waving them out. ''Remember this, and remember it good. I, Alber, and no one else, can make you or break you. *No one* but Alber. Don't ever forget it.''

The thugs and minor officials as well as Mime leave. The beaten man is set on his feet and half-helped, half-dragged along.

Alber turns to Wotan and Logi, and looks at them long and distrustfully. ''Now. What the hell do the sovereigns want in Nibelung?''

''We have heard much of the wonders of production and organization you are working here,'' Wotan says, ''and, anxious always to learn more of the things men hold dear, we have come to see for ourselves.''

Alber is scornful. ''It was simply envy of the things I have gained that has brought you here, so don't imply any noble ideals.''

Logi, attempting to set the tone of the conversation, says, ''I have conferred with your attorneys here frequently, both on matters of criminal and civil law, and without knowing it you have doubtless benefited from some of my advice. I studied law in FAFNER when you were there, studied history of the twentieth century with Mime at the U, and worked with him on the world treaty when Donner upheld his old orders as commander of the UN.''

''But now you find the company of the sovereigns to your liking,'' Alber sneers. ''If you are as false to them as you were to FAFNER, then they have no reason to cherish your company. And if you have given advice to the State's attorneys in Nibelung, I'd better have everything you have been connected with gone over damned carefully.''

''Is that a professional or personal criticism?'' Logi asks.

''I distrust all lawyers on the basis of their profession. And I distrust you in all ways. But,'' he takes a defiant attitude, ''I dare everyone — sovereigns, gods, or schemers. Call yourself what you like but call your shots carefully when you go up against Alber.''

Logi comments dispassionately, ''You are growing bold with power, Alber. And admittedly your power is becoming great. Nibelung is no longer recognizable as a country of the wilds.''

''Have you noticed the way the people dress on the streets?''

LOGE. A richer pile I have never seen.

ALBERICH. That is just today's miserable sight. Tomorrow it will be far bigger.

WOTAN. But what good is wealth in joyless Nibelhelm, where there is nothing of value to buy.

ALBERICH. For gaining riches to raise me up, I need Nibelhelm's night. But with the hoard, that I keep in the hollows, I plan to accomplish wonders. In the end the whole world will know me as its master.

WOTAN. How do you plan to accomplish that feat?

ALBERICH. You who live above in joy, laughter and love, I'll grasp and control you with a hand of gold. As I forswore love, all who live will forswear it. Lured by my gold, gold alone will be the thing for which they strive. You live on radiant heights in visions of rapture. You who know only joy, look down on us dwarfs with disdain. But beware, beware. First your men will work under my power, then your fair women, who spurn my wooing, the dwarf will lure to satisfy his needs — no matter that love is lacking. *(He laughs savagely.)* You have heard, now remember. Beware! Beware the night-born hosts when the Nibelung hoard shall rise from night and darkness into the day.

Alber asks, pleased at having his accomplishments acknowledged. "And have you looked at the stuff offered for sale in the stores?"

Logi admits, "In the capital the wealth rivals some cities of FAFNER and FASOLT."

"Just a frontier village," Alber brags. "Wait until production really starts rolling. Then you'll see wealth that'll turn you green with envy."

"But what is gained," Wotan asks, "by all the factories and the frenzied production? The people were happier without it. And you have enough to indulge every personal whim and wallow in sensual satiety."

"I have enough," Alber admits, "to know that wealth has little value in itself. But the *desire* for wealth, when wealth is dangled before their eyes with artful cleverness, drives men to madness in their scramble to gain it. And madmen are my meat. I have forsworn love and learned how to make use of madmen. I have no ideals. I manipulate their madness to my own advantage by giving them some power and playing madmen against each other — with my own hand ready to take the power from any man when he begins to think it's his own. The maddest of madmen I pick for my own use from out of the general public. Because I keep my eye on the ring, I now have Nibelung in my grasp. Tomorrow I'll have the entire world."

Wotan tells him, "There's a long jump from ruling Nibelung to ruling the world."

Alber laughs disdainfully. "Not so long as you think. You sovereigns think you're made of different clay from all who play the old game of power politics. You lead by impressing people with the beauty and nobility of your ideals. But you, too, have a hidden hunger for something that can be made into the coin of the realm — something that gives you a chance at grabbing the ring. Haven't you already compromised your ideals to gain an impressive city? And you still tell yourselves that your integrity is intact. As I forswore love of all else for the power behind controlled wealth so shall you. No obscure inner sense of beauty, of love, and of nobility can stand in the market place alongside sparkling material splendor without losing by the comparison. And this material splendor is gained by skill in manipulating money, position, or any other status symbol — whatever is the coin of the realm. Controlled wealth is unbeatable power. You can't fight it by inspiring warriors to big ideals for which men are ready to die. First your men will unbuckle their swords in exchange for

WOTAN. *(furiously)* Avaunt, impious fool!

ALBERICH. What does he say?

LOGE. *(stepping between them — to Wotan)* Don't be foolish. *(To Alberich.)* Looking on what you can accomplish, we cannot help but stand in wonder. If your treasure can do everything you say, I must admit you will be the mightiest man alive. The moon and stars, and even the sun in its splendor, would surely look upon you as their master. But what seems of most importance is that those who heap up your gold and add to your power fail to hate you. When your hand held forth the ring, the people held you in awe. But suppose while you were asleep, a thief stole the ring. How then would you save yourself?

ALBERICH. Loge thinks he's very smart and everyone else is a fool. If I had asked him for advice or aid, the thief would be very happy. The helmet-that-hides I, myself, designed. The skillfullest workman, Mime, made it so that I am able to assume any form that I choose. None can see me but I am always there. So, fearing nothing, I am safe even from you my kind, careful friends.

the right to take a hand in the money grabbing game — where I am their master. Then when the game played for gold is the only game that gives prestige, I will have my will with your women who think they're too good for me now. Your women, who think they're so damned high and gorgeous, will see that a realist like me is a more advantageous choice than an idealist like you." He is carried away with his projected plans and laughs defiantly. "Mark my words and beware! Beware the power that grows deep down under cover of darkness. It will ensnare and destroy the idealistic young warriors whose swords flash too conspicuously in the light."

"Avaunt, impious fool!" Wotan explodes.

"What did he say?" Alber asks of Logi.

Logi first says to Wotan, "Don't be foolish now." He then turns to Alber, "It is indeed something at which to marvel, the power to manipulate that controlled money and a controlled media give. I have studied with amazement how your kind used the combination before the big war to surreptitiously get control of FAFNER and FASOLT and the splendor of their cities. The giants have become decadent now and are beginning to look with envy on the skill and vigor shown by Alber in Nibelung. It is not difficult for me to imagine that if you continue on your present path they too, like Nibelung, will fall under your power without a struggle. That is the great marvel of the system: Those it conquers submit as if they were hypnotized. Those who fall under your power, produce the very wealth that gives the power into your hands, and themselves mold of it the fetters that bind them. Then men who were once strong seem to know only fear and all bow and serve what, if they saw clearly, would be the thing most hated. Since this power that you have is not identified with you, since it is a thing apart from you that you hold and wield, do you not live in constant fear that it will be stolen?"

Alber answers, "You, Logi, who walk with the sovereigns yet have colleagues throughout the world, think you are cunning and all men fools. But let me set you right. You sovereigns identify yourselves with your ideals, principles, codes of conduct, and concepts of honor. Then you must live for them and die for them — you can't compromise when the going gets rough. But I am identified with *nothing*. I can support or opppose any movement, any time, anywhere, as befits the moment. I have an invisible place under a banner of equality, fraternity, and the common good. I am just one of many, a common citizen. It is

LOGE. I have seen many marvelous things. But nothing so marvelous as this have I yet seen. I can hardly believe such an unequaled achievement. But if it were possible, your power would be boundless.

ALBERICH. Do you think that I lie and make unfounded claims like Loge?

LOGE. Until it is proved, I will doubt your word.

ALBERICH. Puffed up with his own claim to wisdom, the fool will soon explode. Then, die of envy. Now tell me, what form do you want me to take?

LOGE. Whatever form you choose, but strike me dumb with amazement.

ALBERICH. *(putting on the Tarnhelm)* "Dreaded dragon, appear here."

(Alberich instantly disappears and in his place there writhes a huge monster serpent which bends and opens its outstretched jaws at Wotan and Loge.)

LOGE. *(affecting screaming terror)* Oho! Oho! Horrible dragon, please don't swallow me. Spare the life of poor Loge!

the people who rule, the people who make mistakes — and the *people* who get punished. But though you don't see me I am there, the invisible power — hidden, safe, fearing nothing. And I need not fear you and Wotan. Even if you sat in my chair, had title to all I own, had my secret files and my contracts, you couldn't use them. You are prohibited by your foolish pride from pulling strings in the darkness. You want to stand boldly on a mountain top and let the full light shine on your glorious integration of beauty, noble ideals, and honor."

Logi comments, "If the only values are power and the manipulation of power, then there is much to be said for gold and the things it stands for as a substitute for the natural prime movers of man in their pristine purity."

"You admit my system's value, but you appear unimpressed. Do you think there is some final test other than power? Or do you think my power has an undiscovered weakness?"

"On both points," Logi says, "until proven otherwise by eternity, I seem destined to look for a practical answer."

"You will look in vain," Alber tells him. "The system is flawless; my power is complete. And it takes whatever form I will it."

He presses a button and the drapes, hiding the life-size television, part and the television shows a scene in a department store with a close-up of a clerk showing sheer night gowns to a customer.

"See," he says, my power has all the tender persuasiveness of a woman's touch."

The scene is followed by a commercial for some spray-can product promising an exquisite evening of romance. Then an advertisement for finger control household appliances.

"Or the dreams and ideals for a more beautiful and easier life. Or what form do you like your power to take?"

He pushes a button and shows a scene of police with night sticks wading into and dispersing a political rally.

"You are making an excellent showing," Logi encourages. "Continue. You amaze me."

Alber switches again to a scene of a military parade. Long swords but no guns. Infantry, cavalry, jeeps, motorcycles, trucks. He says, "Now here is something Wotan can appreciate. His warriors have not attacked Nibelung in years now, and with better cause every year."

"Ah, I see," Logi encourages. Alber laughs triumphantly.

WOTAN. *(laughing)* Good, Alberich! Good — and artful. Very swiftly grew the dwarf into an immense dragon.

(The dragon disappears and instead Alberich is seen in his own form.)

ALBERICH. Hehe! You scoffers, are you now convinced?

LOGE. My trembling surely shows how much I was impressed. From what I have seen, I must surely credit the wonder. But just as you immediately turned into something so big, could you also turn into something very small. For slipping away from foes that pressed hard upon you, it might be better to become extremely small. That, though, might be a feat too difficult to perform.

ALBERICH. Too difficult for such as you, maybe. How small shall I become?

LOGE. So small that a tiny crevice could hold you such as a toad slinks into.

ALBERICH. Nothing simpler! Look at me now. *(He puts the Tarnhelm on his head again.)* "Crooked toad, appear here."

(Alberich disappears and in his place there is a toad crawling on the rocks.)

LOGE. *(to Wotan)* Quick and catch it! Capture the toad!

(Wotan sets his foot on the toad. Loge makes a dash at its head and grabs the Tarnhelm.)

ALBERICH. *(is immediately seen in his own form writhing under Wotan's foot.)* Ohe! I'm caught. My curse on my captors.

LOGE. Hold him fast until he is tied.

(Loge binds Alberich hand and foot with a rope.)

LOGE. Now he is ours. Let's go back up.

(They take the prisoner, who struggles furiously, and drag him with them through the opening from which they came down and exit, going upwards.)

Logi goes on, "I have heard that you have developed a formidable force. This sampling is very impressive."

"Well-trained men," Wotan says. "I hear you are strong on organization and discipline."

"Are you convinced?" Alber asks. "That is power as you understand it. I have the biggest and best equipped armies in the world. Of course, I except the cities of FAFNER and FASOLT, where more than cold steel is permitted by treaty. But now I might even have a chance against them. My armies are machines; they respond unquestioningly to my control. I don't have warriors like yours, sovereigns inspired by ideals, who fight only for what they believe. My men are drafted for the protection of the common good — and I decide what is the common good. They serve only because it's more healthy to serve. They are branded as cowards and traitors if they don't. If they do they get good pay and the finest of everything."

Logi fills in, "And you command all by casually issued orders, a word here and a word there in the right places. Only those receiving them need know the full power of Alber. And they are removed if they learn too little or too much."

Alber switches off the television and settles comfortably in a chair at his desk. "Nothing simpler!" he says. "Three girls once called me a frog, a harmless lovesick frog. Who would harm a poor toad? I am just a poor, overworked, weary businessman who sometimes helps in his humble way to throw unscrupulous politicians out of office and replace them with public minded statesmen."

The door is thrown open to admit the five thugs, with their hands tied, in the custody of four of Wotan's warriors. The warriors are dressed as the guard was in chapter II. Mime is also there, untied but clearly in custody. Alber reaches for the intercom but his hand is knocked against the desk and rendered helpless by a blow from Wotan.

"Quick, catch it!" Logi says to a warrior. "That toad in men's clothing."

The warrior leaps over behind Alber and places his knife point at Alber's throat.

Alber's eyes rove the room while he is careful not to provoke the guard behind him, "My boys, and my stupid stooge, Mime. And now I am caught! What in hell's going on here?"

"You will hear in good time," Logi tells him, "and speak a few well-chosen words in the right places."

FOURTH SCENE

The scene changes in the same manner as before, but in the reverse order. Open space on a mountain top as in the second scene, veiled in a pale mist. Wotan and Loge climb up from the cavern, bringing with them Alberich, who is still bound.

LOGE. Here, kinsman, be seated. Look, behold, there lies the world that you long so to bend to your will. What corner, say, will you give me for my stall.

ALBERICH. Infamous scoundrel! Loosen my bonds, or you'll answer dearly for this outrage.

WOTAN. You are my captive, caught and in fetters. You subdued the world and thought it was yours. Now you lie at my feet in fetters. Before letting you loose, a ransom we want.

ALBERICH. What a stupid fool I've been — to blindly trust a treacherous thief! I'll think up a fearful revenge for this wrong.

IV

After a little shifting about, positions now suggest a radically different happening than a few minutes before. Alber's thugs have been released and stationed where they cannot leave the room without running into Wotan's warriors. Two additional warriors have been brought in. Wotan, Logi, Alber and Mime have taken positions that give the assembly an appearance of being a high level conference attended by Wotan with an honor guard. At first, however, the conversation is still informal.

"Alber," Logi begins, "we were once fellow segments of the same tera. I must admit I don't cherish the old school bond but we are going to give the appearance of being your guests in Nibelung for awhile. I will assume again the status of your fellow segment — or I should say *citizen* since we'll now be speaking your language. Yes, and I must remember to say "state" not "tera." I must have the full confidence of all your associates as your former compatriot and trusted new attorney. Wotan and his personal escort of warriors are to be received by the highest dignitaries as honored guests of the state. Vague, veiled rumors will leak out that a political alliance very favorable to Nibelung may be in the making."

"You god-damned stupid fools!" Alber answers. "Do you think you can get by with this? Call it a joke and get out of Nibelung while you still can. Fail to do that and you'll all regret the day you were born."

Wotan tells him, "You are my captive as are your boys who will always stand by to give an impression that all is well. And now I show you the weakness of your system. You care nothing for honor; you value only your worthless life; and to save that life you will pay any price."

"I can see I was a fool to sit with you in friendly discussion while you bound my boys and accomplished this treachery," Alber says. "But don't let it go to your head. I'll have my revenge and I'll think up a good one. You would have attacked Nibelung long ago if you had dared. I am ready to attack the sovereigns right now, and *I* dare. You have always known it would have been only

83

LOGE. Before you think of revenge, you'd better think of how to win your freedom. No freeman fears revenge from one who is tied hand and foot. So before you think of vengeance, think first of ransom.

ALBERICH. Then state your demands.

WOTAN. The hoard of gleaming gold.

ALBERICH. You pair of unscrupulous thieves! *(aside)* If I can keep the ring, the hoard I can readily yield. For I can get this much and still more by the use of the ring. If this experience serves as a warning to make me more wise, what I lose here is a cheap payment for it.

WOTAN. Will you yield up the hoard?

ALBERICH. Untie my hand. I'll summon it here.

(Loge unties his right hand.)

ALBERICH. *(touches the ring with his lips and secretly murmurs a command.)* Now then, I have called up the Nibelung crew. You'll soon see them coming, obeying their master. Now loosen these burdensome bonds.

WOTAN. Wait for that. We'll get the payment first.

(The Nibelungs climb up from the crevice ladened with the treasure that makes up the hoard.)

ALBERICH. This bitter disgrace — that my shrinking slaves can see me bound as a captive. — There, as I tell you! Pile up the hoard. And keep your eyes on your work. Don't look around at me. Quick there — quick. Get the job done and get back to your tunnels. I'll be coming after you right away.

a matter of time anyway."

Logi says, "An ambitious dream and one we know has been yours a long time. Also, now that the sovereigns have a city, a center of operation and a tangible symbol of prestige, we know we are more vulnerable. But before you have your vengeance you must be safe from the sharp swords of sovereign warriors who everywhere surround you. So forget vengeance for now and talk of ransom."

"O.K. Get on with it. Let's hear your god-damned demands."

"Everything you have," Wotan tells him. "You will give Logi full power of attorney in all your affairs."

"Full power of attorney?" Alber questions in disbelief. "What the hell good can that do you? I have mines, factories, lands, office buildings, houses, whole cities, but you can't simply carry them away. You might liquidate some and come up with a few million in cash but that would mean nothing to the sovereigns. Do you propose to become citizens of Nibelung — segments of teras, dwarfs, or zombis as you call us? And will you run in the next elections for high office?" He laughs at the ridiculousness of it and taunts, "Have you already got your own political machine all oiled up and running?"

Wotan asks, "Will you give Logi full power of attorney — or do we announce that you have had your throat cut?"

"O.K. I'll call a stenographer. He can dictate the document."

Wotan nods permission and Alber reaches for the intercom but Logi interrupts him. "We have much to do in the next few months and might as well get started. Call in your stockbroker, your banker, your executive staff and introduce us. Here is what you will say." Logi hands him a paper, then, while he is reading it, adds, "Also tell your secretary to bring in your appointment book."

As Alber reaches again for the intercom, Wotan nods to a guard who puts a knife at his throat. He talks in a low voice into the intercom, then turns it off and says to Wotan and Logi, "Someone will get wise to this game."

"If they do your life is the forfeit," Wotan tells him.

The staff assembles in the office. Alber rises and addresses them ceremoniously, "You have the unprecedented honor of meeting Wotan, leader of the sovereigns, perhaps better known to you as Chief of the Gods."

There is a wave of awe, confusion, obvious elation, a few shouts of "Long live Wotan" and deep curtsies by some of the

(The Nibelungs pile up the hoard, and quickly slip back into the cleft.)

ALBERICH. I've paid what you asked. Now let me go. And that helmet there, that Loge has, please be kind enough to give it back to me.

LOGE. *(throwing the Tarnhelm on the heap)* We take it as part of the plunder.

ALBERICH. Accursed thief! — But patience, be calm. He who fashioned it for me can make me another. Mine is still the might that Mime will obey. But it is a setback that I must now leave my subtle defense to my enemies. — Now then, everything has been taken from Alberich. He now owns nothing. So release his bonds.

secretaries.

Wotan bows and says, "I am deeply moved by your greeting. Thank you."

Alber continues the formal address: "I have been invited by the President to attend a high level conference between Nibelung and the sovereigns which will last some time. Meanwhile, I have brought in the one person to whom I can fully entrust my affairs, my old childhood friend who is a most able lawyer, Mr. Logi. I am giving him full power of attorney. As important events between Nibelung and the sovereigns may be in the making, don't be surprised by anything he may do. I will be in touch with him and he has my complete confidence. Let him have any information he may seek and give him your complete cooperation. That is all, thank you."

The staff leave, still showing great respect for Wotan. One secretary finds time in passing for a quick flirtation with one of Wotan's warriors.

When the door is closed Alber says, "Now that's over — a clever little maneuver. As I get it the conference with the President will be nothing but a routine event honoring Wotan's visit to Nibelung. I assume it's just an excuse for you to hold me away from here while Logi makes free with my holdings. You can't actually be thinking of entering Nibelung's politics?"

"For several months now," Logi says, "hidden by the concept that men can be reduced to ciphers, I have made a study of Nibelung's politics and observed the fine hand of Mime at work. He is too cautious for a final showdown, but his priming is very thorough and includes his own man as Vice President. Your President is going to resign because of ill health and take a trip into the wilds. The Vice President will take over."

Mime shows great joy, "I will gladly help in this plan. My good intentions have always been misinterpreted. I have been an enemy only to the falseness of Alber."

"Mime!" Alber says, "I should have cut you in little pieces and flushed you down the sewer long ago but you are such a cautious god-damned ass I can forget you. Wotan, you are the one that is hard to figure in this deal. You sovereigns can't rule Nibelung through my political machine without being always on the scene, and none of you can remain and become identified with this kind of politics. Standard politics violate everything you stand for — they violate all those stupid romantic dreams of honor on which you build your power. When I'm free I'll rise again. I know

87

LOGE. *(to Wotan)* Are you satisfied. Shall I untie him.

WOTAN. A golden ring remains on his finger. That also belongs on the hoard.

ALBERICH. *(horrified)* The ring!

WOTAN. The ring also is part of the ransom.

ALBERICH. You can take my life — but you can't have the ring!

WOTAN. It's the ring I want. I'm not interested in your life.

ALBERICH. If my life and limbs you leave me, I must also have the ring. Eye and ear, head and hand, are not mine more surely than this ring.

WOTAN. The ring you claim as your own. Where did you get the substance from which to fashion it? Was it yours — that, which from the water's depth you tore away. Go ask the Rhinemaidens how you got the Rhinegold from which to make the ring. You took it by theft.

ALBERICH. Such vile double dealing! Such shameless deceit! You, a robber, reproach me for the thing you were dying to do. You would readily have stolen the Rhinegold if it had been as easy to forge as to steal. So, hypocrite, how happy you are that the Nibelung, here, in tortured need, in a maddened moment, won the terrible magic that you now find so attractive. Shall I, debarred from bliss, and burdened by anguish, grant my ring as an ornament to you for your pleasure — my ban bringing blessings to you? Arrogant god, look to what you're doing. The ring's evil now falls on me alone. But on all things that have been, that are, and that will be, this evil will strike if you are rash enough to seize the ring.

WOTAN. Yield the ring! You win no right to keep it by reason of your foolish talk.

I'm going to pay through the nose now. That doesn't bug me much. All I want to know is: When do I get my freedom?''

Logi interrupts Alber by speaking to Wotan, "Do we need to agree on anything more before the reception at the capital?''

Wotan says, "Public opinion must be watched early. Publicity on the reception must not go wrong. Mime must be appointed minister of propaganda immediately, and he will act under my personal control.''

Mime gestures his joy.

Alber becomes more disturbed than ever before and says, "You can have my life before I consent to that. And you know that if you liquidate me your game will fall apart.''

Wotan looks at him with contempt, "An idle gesture that — pretending something is dearer than saving your skin. I know the dwarf I hold under the foot I'd like to stomp down on with all the weight I've got.''

Alber persists, "I operated factories at a loss for years to get television receivers as widely distributed as possible. The flow of the people's ambitions and desires is my very life blood.''

Wotan answers, "You claim it as yours, but what do you claim? Men's ideals? Men's dreams? Have you ever contributed to their stature? Never. Just the contrary. Playing one against the other to keep all impotent has been the sole purpose of your efforts. Your propaganda has been used to create zombis with no dreams whatsoever or to make men dwarfs and their dreams dwarf size. Even when considering the material things, the desire for which you use to make men slaves, yours was not the art that designed them nor the work that produced them. And title to the raw materials you obtained by theft.''

"Of all the duplicity yours is the worst,'' Alber comes back. "You put me down for being a thief, even while you hold me captive and steal from me. And for what greater duplicity than theft do you reproach me? Merely the act of encouraging a desire for material wealth — a desire that in yourself you indulge without shame, first bargaining for grandeur with the teras and now stealing the fruits of my labors — or my duplicity — as you look at it. You disdain my methods but you think you can reap the fruits of those methods without harm. Watch yourself, arrogant god! The fruit still bears in itself the taint of the vine that produced it.''

"Enough of this talk,'' Wotan brushes it aside. "When we go to the capital you will advise the President that there should be no news release until the new propaganda minister is appointed

ALBERICH. *(screaming horribly)* Weh! I'm defeated. Destroyed. A slave to the vilest of slaves.

WOTAN. *(putting the ring on his finger and contemplating it with satisfaction)* I own what makes me supreme, the mightiest monarch of all.

LOGE. *(to Wotan)* Shall I release him.

WOTAN. Set him loose.

LOGE. *(undoing Alberich's bonds)* You can go home now. No shackles hold you. You are free.

ALBERICH. Am I now free — really free? Then take my freedom's first salute. As at first by a curse the ring was fashioned, the curse goes with the ring. May the magic of the gold, which gave measureless might to me, forever deal death to its owner. No man shall gain gladness from its possession. May ill-fortune follow its owner, and envy be the lot of all who see that others have it. All shall crave after its delights, but none shall be happy who has it. Murder shall go where its owner goes. The coward, death-doomed, shall be bound by its fetters. Through his whole life, the treasure's owner shall be the treasure's slave, until, within my hand, I once more hold it. So — in bitter despair, the Nibelung blesses his ring. I give it to you. Guard it with care. But the curse that goes with it, you cannot avoid. *(He vanishes quickly into the cleft.)*

and has a chance to talk to his agency."

Alber glares from one to the other and says resignedly, "Beaten at my own game! And by a bunch of romantic fools! It can't happen this way. It *can't. How the hell* did I get in a mess like this?"

Wotan tells Mime, "The news release will say only that the sovereigns have arrived and are conferring with state officials on matters of great importance. I'll give you further instructions later."

Logi asks, "Are we ready?"

"That's everything," Wotan tells him. "Alber can be freed when the full task is accomplished."

Logi turns to Alber, "You know the meaning of Wotan's word. Again you will be an outcast with a second chance to become a free man or to again play the dwarf's game of teras and zombis. Which will it be?"

"Which do you think?" Alber grins sardonically.

Wotan shows intention of leaving. Alber remains immovable. Wotan nods to a guard at whose approach Alber rises, but instead of leaving he turns to Wotan with great seriousness and says:

"Having lost all else I've got nothing left but my hate! But let me tell you something about visions in a night of hate. My hate gives me some dreams now, dreams of the god writhing in torment. I see visions now of your terrible downfall. That will be a downfall such as you can't even imagine. Do you know what will happen when you, a romantic idealist, begin trying to control *and shape* the thoughts and opinions of the whole vulgar populace? That, let me tell you, is something a lot different from leading people who are eager to follow your leadership because they see and like where you're going. This is the old Ring game. Do you hear me? The old Ring game! From this game no man can have joy. A curse rides with it forever. Even among the state officials of FASOLT and FAFNER, tired old men who have become nothing but figureheads, there is anguish and torment like you could never believe. Those in control are gnawed constantly by fearful envy and, in fact just as in symbol, they have found that the only reward for each coveted position is a self-devouring serpent. That alone should turn you away. But listen to this: The curse is in proportion to the stature of the accursed Ring's holder! In the teras of our time the manipulators of public opinion have played only with pompous parades of their positions — and could lose only that coveted pomp. I — who am undoubtedly the master

LOGE. Did you hear his fond farewell?

WOTAN. *(absorbed in contemplating the ring)* Don't grudge him vent to his spleen.

manipulator — have played only with power and could suffer only the loss of power. But you claim greatness and for you the curse will be great. You play with an ideal that to you is more than life, and so after losing it, still, in honor, you must live when life is less than worthless. The arrogant god I will yet see crawl. When you hold the Ring you will find yourself committed to the ways of a cringing coward — death-doomed but unable to welcome death." He laughs with malevolence then concludes, "Mark my words and start learning to walk with fear even now."

Logi asks Wotan, "Do you find a measure of truth in his words?"

Wotan is making notes for the coming broadcast and paying little attention to Alber. In answer to Logi, he says only, "Don't grudge him vent for his spleen!"

(The vapor in the foreground now gradually clears.)

LOGE. *(looking to the right)* Fasolt and Fafner are coming in the distance. Freia is coming with them.

(From the other side enter Fricka, Donner, and Froh.)

FROH. They return.

DONNER. We greet you, brother.

FRICKA. Do you bring good news?

LOGE. *(pointing to the hoard)* By fraud and by force, we got what we sought. There is Freia's ransom.

DONNER. She is now hurrying toward us from the giant's hold.

FROH. The exquisite air gladdens us again. It is a wonderful feeling. Sad would have been our lot, if she who gives us youth and lasting delights had been withheld from us forever.

(The foreground is now quite clear again. The light restores the gods to their original freshness. The background, however, is still veiled in mist, so that the castle is not visible.)

(Fasolt and Fafner enter, leading Freia.)

FRICKA. *(hastening joyfully to Freia, seeking to embrace her)* Loveliest sister. Sweetest delight. Once more you can be among us.

FASOLT. *(stopping her)* Halt! Don't touch her yet. Freia is still ours. On Reisenheim's rocky rampart we held the captive, and treated her with respectful care. It is with deep regret that we bring her back in case you have her ransom.

V

Six months later a similar but more luxurious and ornate room at the capital of Nibelung is the focus of world affairs. Logi, Wotan, and Nibelung's President, a figurehead politician, are awaiting the arrival of negotiators for a new treaty between the sovereigns and teras. Fricka and Donner arrive first and are met by a silent embrace and handclasp from Wotan. Wotan is thoughtful and shows no inclination to talk.

Logi tells the new arrivals, "FASOLT's and FAFNER's representatives are due any moment. You have barely arrived in time for the conference."

Donner, as usual unfriendly toward Logi says, "I suppose you have ensnared the sovereigns again."

Fricka is a little more friendly and includes Logi in asking both him and Wotan, "Has everything gone well?"

Logi answers, "We could hold our own limited boundaries inviolate by meeting all the conditions the teras have already set. I have hopes that Wotan won't have to concede all they ask."

Donner thaws a little and says, "But even if he must, there will still be one island of freedom left in the world. That, at least, is something." He even adds with an indulgent smile at himself, "My feeling now is what it always was at the end of each long drama — Freia and Froh again together, youth everlasting, bruised and in tatters but still triumphant over darkness and pain. I guess I actually am a romantic."

Fricka shows her understanding by saying, "I feel as if my own sister had already been abducted and today may be restored to me."

FASOLT's and FAFNER's representatives are shown in by sovereign guards. There are stiff formal bows and all gather around the conference table. Sovereign guards stand by.

FASOLT's representative hurries to assert himself, "We are meeting again as agreed and I trust you have observed that our nations, trying as always to be just, have been particularly diligent during the last six months to keep down the grosser elements from

WOTAN. The ransom is ready at hand. It must be carefully measured.

FASOLT. It will make me very sad to lose the maiden. In order for me to forget her, the sparkling hoard must be heaped in a stack high enough to hide the heavenly maid from our sight.

WOTAN. Let Freia's form be the gauge of gold.

(Fasolt and Fafner place Freia in the middle of the stage. They stick their staves into the ground on each side, so as to give the measure of her height and breadth.)

FAFNER. We have planted our poles in proper form. Pile up the hoard high to this measure.

WOTAN. Hurry up with the task. It is a hateful business.

LOGE. Help me, Froh.

FROH. Freia's shame, I'll quickly erase.

(Loge and Froh quickly heap up the treasure between the poles.)

FAFNER. Don't make the pile so light and loose. Pack the gauge firm and close. *(He roughly presses the treasure closer together and stoops to look at it for crevices.)* Through here I can see light. All chinks must be hidden.

LOGE. Hands off, you bungler, let it alone.

FAFNER. Look here, This gap must be closed.

WOTAN. *(turning away moodily)* Deep in my breast burns this awful shame. *(His eyes are fixed on Freia.)*

their abductions. We wanted to be sure we could not be accused of taking in advance what is to be yours by this treaty — if you are able to meet the agreed terms."

Wotan answers stiffly, "We are ready. The administration of Nibelung is efficient and can easily be passed to your control."

FASOLT's representative is obviously enjoying the process of bargaining when he is on the side with all the advantages. He says, "My people will be grieved by this turn of events. They were looking forward to a complete and savory synthesis of all our cultures under the broad banner of brotherhood for all mankind. We can make no minor concessions to add to their bitter disappointment."

Wotan answers with contempt, "We are not here to quibble. We will concede the natural geography as being the true boundaries of Nibelung."

FAFNER's representative realizes that, without a formal opening, negotiations have actually started and injects a question, "And the title to the mineral lands where the population is nomad and acknowledges no government?"

"All the way to the sea," Wotan snaps. "Let's get on with it. This is foul business at best and it gags me."

Logi takes over, "I know the intention and have drawn the description." He lays the contract and maps before them.

Feeling the power that they represent, as if they, themselves, were the phantom giants sitting at the table, the representatives of FASOLT and FAFNER look over the maps and the contract's wording.

FAFNER's representative says, "Here, this clause is ambiguous. It could be construed as giving to the teras jointly the disputed area between FAFNER and Nibelung that rightfully belongs to FAFNER now." He starts to make correction with his pen.

Logi says, "I had some uncertainty on that point. Mark it but leave it alone; I'll change the wording."

"And here," FAFNER's representative points out, "The extent of territorial waters in this area must be defined."

Wotan leaves the table and turns his back on the conference in emotional repulsion. He speaks his thoughts aloud, to everyone and to no one, "Deep against my heart burns this disgrace. To hold our own little island of freedom we are agreeing to use no force against those who do their *bloody* work in darkness so that in daylight they can *verbally* control people brainwashed into conformity."

FRICKA. Look at the beautiful Freia standing there in shame. Without a word, she pleads with her eyes. Heartless man! Our lovely maid owes her present position to your doing.

FAFNER. Still more must be piled on.

DONNER. This is too much. My rage grows hot. Roused by this insolent rogue. Come here, you hound. You want to measure! Measure your strength against mine.

FAFNER. Softly, Donner! Your roaring is out of place. There is no need for it here.

DONNER. *(laughing at him)* I could crush you into little pieces.

WOTAN. Be calm. I think Freia is hid.

LOGE. The hoard gives out.

FAFNER. *(measuring with his eye)* I can still see Holda's hair. Throw that woven work on the heap.

LOGE. What! Even the Tarnhelm.

FAFNER. Hurry it up. Put it here.

WOTAN. Let it go, also.

LOGE. *(throwing the Tarnhelm on the heap)* At last we have finished. Have you enough now.

FASOLT. Freia the glorious is hidden forever. The ransom has been paid and I have lost her. *(He goes nearer and peers through the hoard.)* Ah! Her glance still gleams on me here. Through this chink I can still see her eyes. While her beautiful eyes I behold, I cannot leave the goddess.

Fricka gets up from the table and comes to his side, saying, "Even though our country is insignificant in size when you look at maps of the world, remember there are many women in Godsland. They are looking helplessly to you for security."

FAFNER's representative continues to scrutinize the maps and treaty, "Here! These islands! They must be included."

Donner turns on him, "Treaties! Treaties! Words! Words! You want to measure the last grain of sand on the beach. If you are so precise with measurements, weigh your bombs against those of the sovereigns."

FAFNER's representative pushes back the maps a minute and glares defiantly at him, "I know, as well as you, to the last ounce how much explosives were left in the world when their manufacture was outlawed. And I know the range and scope of every missile."

Donner: "Then you know FAFNER would disappear in twenty-three quick flashes if we could tear up the treaties."

Wotan goes back to the table saying, "Calm yourselves, agreement can be reached."

Logi tells Wotan, "The boundaries of Nibelung are established."

FAFNER's representative addresses Wotan, "Now can you assure us that the President and the governing body will approve annexation to the Nations' Protective League and offer no resistance to our occupation police forces?"

Logi answers, "The decision of the governing body is subject to ratification by popular vote."

"What is this!" FAFNER's representative explodes. "Have you been wasting our time?"

Wotan injects, "The governing body's vote is adequately controlled. Here is the President; let him answer for the people."

The President says, "There must be popular ratification on an action of this kind or it is invalid in six months. But meanwhile your occupation police will have taken control. By the time for the popular vote the word will have been passed through enough cooperative groups in both labor and industry to assure the election's success."

Logi concludes, "I think the terms can be considered satisfactory now and the final treaty can be prepared for signature."

FASOLT's representative recognizes the opportunity for oratory again and begins, "My dream of free commerce and free passage for all the people of the world, my dream of seeing all mankind united into one harmonious family has suffered much

FAFNER. Ha! You hear me? This chink must be stopped.

LOGE. You're never sated. Can't you see the gold is all gone.

FAFNER. By no means, friend. There is a ring on Wotan's finger. Give that to close up the crevice.

WOTAN. What! Give up the ring?

LOGE. Let me counsel you. The gold belongs to the Rhine-maidens. Wotan will return to them what is theirs.

WOTAN. You talk nonsense. The ring that I won with great effort, unawed, I'll keep for myself.

LOGE. Then the promise that I gave to the Rhine-maidens will be broken.

WOTAN. I am not bound by your promises. I won the ring so it is mine.

FAFNER. Not so. The ring is part of the ransom.

WOTAN. Ask what else you will. But not for all the world will I give you the ring.

FASOLT. *(pulls Freia from behind the hoard.)* All is off. The original bargain stands. Fair Freia is ours forever.

FREIA. Help me! Help me!

FRICKA. Heartless god. Give it to them. Let them have their way.

FROH. Don't hold it back.

by this treaty. This defeat to the cause will give our next educational campaign a great additional obstacle to overcome."

"Educational campaign? That's right," FAFNER's representative agrees. "But why can't you say things straight in your own language. The question of TV propaganda control must be settled."

Logi tells him, "We cannot by contract agree upon what you can lead the people to believe."

"True," FAFNER's representative answers. "But Wotan has a faithful following in Nibelung — by no means a majority, but they can be troublesome. He has aroused them strongly during the last six months. He has promised that someday a leader will come and show the way to victory. It must be agreed that from this time forward there will never again be a public broadcast by the sovereigns in Nibelung."

"What!" Wotan jumps to his feet. "Our original agreement called for open air receivers for sovereign broadcast throughout the wilds. It is only to move a portion of the battle to the idealogical plane that I make treaties at all."

Logi tries to calm him by saying, "I was drawn to the sovereigns by your ideals. I ask that you don't forget them now. Full freedom for individual self-determination you have always upheld as the basic good. It should not be influenced by any propaganda."

Wotan is unyielding and says, "The sovereigns' broadcast is a thing I have strived for these many years. I *cannot* give that up."

"I have always told everyone that you advocated true freedom. Would you now make me a liar?" Logi asks.

"I have never made you my spokesman," Wotan tells him. "But freedom will be the keynote of our broadcasts."

FAFNER's representative joins in, "You may have your broadcasts elsewhere in the wilds but in delivering Nibelung you deliver all property, including your own open air receivers, and you deliver also television control."

Wotan says, "The physical receiving stations I will concede if you insist but there must be free television. You must not jam my broadcasts."

FAFNER's representative says firmly, "You know I won't give in on that point. If there is free television in Nibelung there will be free passage of people throughout the world."

"Not that, Wotan!" Fricka cries. "The Godsland must not

DONNER. Give them the ring too.

WOTAN. Let me alone. The ring I'll keep.

(Fafner holds back the departing Fasolt. All stand perplexed while Wotan turns away in wrath. The stage has again become dark. From the rocky cleft at the side shines out a bluish glow in which Wotan suddenly perceives Erda, who rises from below so that her upper half is seen. Hers is a noble presence.)

ERDA. *(stretching out her hand warningly toward Wotan)* Yield it, Wotan! Yield it! Avoid the ring's dread curse. Ruin and utter downfall wait for you in its wealth.

WOTAN. What woman speaks such warning words.

ERDA. All things that were I know, and all things that are. All things that shall be I can foresee. The endless world's all-wise one, Erda, seeks to open your eyes. Before the world was made, three daughters were born to me. All my knowledge the Norns tell nightly to Wotan. Now, responding to the direst danger, I, myself, come to your help. Hear me! Hear me! Hear me! A dismal day dawns for the gods. Be warned. Give up the ring.

(Erda sinks slowly as far as the breast and the bluish light begins to fade.)

WOTAN. A mystic might rings in your words. Wait, and tell me more.

ERDA. *(disappearing)* I have warned you. You know enough. Weigh my words wisely. *(She completely disappears.)*

be violated."

"Give up the broadcasts," Donner adds. "You know as well as I that words have no value."

Wotan tenses himself to a more rocklike position as he says, "I must get to men's minds. I must appeal to men's ideals. I will *not* yield the point."

FASOLT's representative makes an ostentatious show of walking out on the conference. He is stopped by FAFNER's; they converse. They go to the door and call in aides with whom they segregate into groups and confer. Logi makes notes on the contracts, talks to the President, calls in clerks and gives them instructions for modifying the contract.

In the confusion a beautiful and impressive woman slips into the room. She is about to be removed by guards (Nibelung guards in cloth uniforms who have followed her into the room) when she pushes them back with a gesture of her arms and addresses the room, "Show me the man who is like a god."

Wotan has been standing in deep thought with his back turned to the commotion in the room. He now turns at the unfamiliar voice and, across the room, she says to him, "Wotan, hear what I have to tell you. All who covet the Ring become less than gods — *and less than men*. Yield it, Wotan, yield it. The teras want it, yield it to them, and let *them* be damned."

"Who are you," Wotan demands, "that you slip into this conference, unknown, and expect me to heed your warning?"

"My name is Erda. My father called me a child of the earth. But names are not important. All that's significant resides in reality. I am a woman and a man should recognize that I hold in my being all things that were, all things that are, and all things that ever shall be. This much only I can tell you in words: The attempt to lead by shaping men's thoughts and ideals is the way to certain destruction. He who would shape man's destiny must work not with minds and emotions but with blood and flesh and bone."

She starts to leave, with the guards accompanying her, then pauses as Wotan says, "You speak a wisdom that I once knew but had almost forgotten. In your words there rings a mystic might that I recognize. Hold a moment and answer this. Is all teaching wrong, even of truth?"

Pushing the guards aside, she turns again and says, "Truth? A *verbal* truth that is grander and better articulated than organic reality? A truth for man that surpasses his blood and being? You have been warned. My words have said all that words can say.

WOTAN. Pain and peril threaten. I must detain you until all is answered.

(He starts for the crevice in order to detain Erda. Donner, Froh, and Fricka throw themselves in his way and hold him back.)

FRICKA. What are you trying to do, madman?

FROH. Take heed, Wotan. Don't seek to hold her. Weigh her words.

DONNER. *(to the giants)* Hear, you giants. Come back and wait. The gold also we'll give you.

FRICKA. Do I dare hope it. Do you deem Holda worth such a price.

(All look anxiously at Wotan. He has been absorbed in deep thought. He now musters his strength to a decision.)

WOTAN. Come back, Freia, you are free. Youth everlasting is ransomed. Here, giants, take the ring. *(He throws the ring on the heap.)*

(The giants release Freia. She hastens joyfully to the gods, who embrace her in turn for some time, with greatest delight.)

FASOLT. *(to Fafner)* Hold on there, don't get greedy. Equally we should share this.

Weigh them wisely." She turns away with finality, a guard opens the door for her, she leaves, followed by the guards.

Wotan says, "That woman has something in her still that now seems missing in me. I must probe the depths of her wisdom."

He starts to leave but Fricka places a restraining hand on him and says, "Don't act like a madman. She is only a woman. I am a woman and I, too, have often warned you: Your ambitions are too great."

Wotan looks at Fricka as if he had never before seen her, he turns away, then confers aside with Logi and Donner.

Donner turns and addresses the teras' representatives who, both, are now preparing for a dramatic walk-out on the conference. "Hear, you teras," he says. "Perhaps your terms will be granted."

Fricka rushes to Wotan and pleads, "You will agree, won't you? You will pay even this price for the safety of our sisters and daughters. Tell me all is not lost."

Logi speaks to the teras' representatives, "The understanding must be clear. Wotan has followers in Nibelung. The sovereigns will not attempt to lead or aid them directly, nor by television broadcasts, nor mass meetings, but Wotan, I, and other sovereigns may enter Nibelung without publicity and observe conditions. There must be no discrimination against those who have proclaimed their sovereignty and shown themselves to be in agreement with Wotan's objectives. They can be cast out from Nibelung but not imprisoned. Also they can leave of their own will if they choose. It is understood that we will give no aid in any battles. But if there should be battles, the sovereigns can come and remove from Nibelung the wounded followers of Wotan's ideals who cannot leave of their own accord."

The giants' representatives glance at each other, shrug and nod assent. All turn and watch Wotan. He ponders long, then comes to a sudden decision and says, "Draw the treaty as stated. The Ring is yours."

FAFNER's and FASOLT's representatives both conspicuously hand notes to aides who depart in great haste. The President of Nibelung leaves with them. The clerks Logi brought in get the treaty ready, then leave. The treaty is laid out on the table and signed by FASOLT's and FAFNER's representatives, and by Wotan.

FASOLT's representative turns to FAFNER's and says, "All broadcast channels in Nibelung should be opened to both our nations. Just as you have done, I, too, have dispatched news of the treaty. Our broadcast will already be on the air; the channel

FAFNER. You were more set on the maid than the gold. You wanted her for yourself, not to share with me. So it seems only fair that most of the gold should be mine.

FASOLT. Swindler and thief. That's the way you play it. *(To the gods)* Come judge between us. Divide the hoard in the way that seems fair to you.

(Wotan turns away in contempt.)

LOGE. Let him have the treasure. Hold on to what matters — the ring.

FASOLT. *(throws himself at Fafner who is packing up the treasure.)* Keep back, you thief. The ring is mine. It veiled Freia's smile from me. *(He hastily snatches the ring.)*

FAFNER. Take your hands off that. The ring is mine.

(There is a struggle. Fasolt gets the ring from Fafner.)

FASOLT. I have it. And I'll keep it.

FAFNER. Hold it fast, or it may fall!

(Fafner furiously hits Fasolt with his staff and with one blow knocks him to the ground. Then from the dying giant he hastily takes the ring.)

FAFNER. Now feast on Freia's smile. You will not again touch the ring.

(He puts the ring into the sack and calmly collects the rest of the gold. All the gods stand horrified. There is a long solemn silence.)

WOTAN. Fearful, indeed, I can see is the curses might.

controls should be opened now.''

"There will be no outside broadcasts," FAFNER's representative counters, "until terms have been worked out. All matters will be administered jointly until further agreements are reached."

FASOLT's representative: "We've been in joint ventures with you before to our sorrow." He turns to the sovereigns, "Wotan, Donner's forces that you command were originally the UN World Police. Sit in now on our conferences and arbitrate, letting Donner's forces give weight to justice as you decree it."

"What!" Wotan explodes. "I ask Donner to help settle your stinking differences? You want me to ask that of a man whom you outlawed because he would not follow your filthy orders?" He turns away in contempt.

FASOLT's representative turns back to FAFNER's who has been busy dispatching messages. "Don't try taking control here now. Our planes are already in the air; a police force will land in a matter of minutes."

FAFNER's representative: "Do you think we have sat idly by? A little police force coming — children's play!"

FASOLT's representative goes to push buttons similar to those on Alber's desk saying, "This official receiver will get outside broadcasts. Let's *see* what's going on."

FAFNER's representative smiles, "Turn it on. I'm anxious to *hear* your planned propaganda and *see* our answer."

The television comes on with news from FASOLT. A news reporter is seen talking, "...and so today Nibelung rises to a world power. FASOLT welcomes the little brother to the family of nations and will give it..." A red light flashes on the screen and a siren screams. "The red alert! Just a moment and I will see if it is a mistake. No! No, it is *not* a mistake. It is *real*! The *black* plan has just been ordered. THIS IS TOTAL WAR! Intercontinental missiles from FAFNER have been in the air more than ten minutes! Look! Look!...No *you* can't see it, but the screens from coast cities are already going black! They flash then go black. I hope *our* missiles were in the air before the hits. Interceptors have been fired by both us and FAFNER but their effectiveness is doubtful. There's no hope but evacuate into the wilds! I'm going! Goodby world! See you in hell!" The screen shows the newscaster dashing out the door. Then silence and an empty studio. Then a blinding flash followed by a black screen.

Wotan, watching, says, "It's no old wife's tale, that legend about the curse's might."

LOGE. Wotan, your luck is unmatched. Your gain was great in getting the ring. But greater still in losing it. Your enemies kill your enemies, fighting over the gold that you let go.

WOTAN. Dark forebodings oppress me! Sickly fears fetter my soul. Erda must tell me how to end them. I will go to her.

FRICKA. *(approaching him coaxingly)* Why linger, Wotan? Wonderously fair are the stately walls. Do they not offer you a genial welcome?

WOTAN. They exacted a shameful price.

DONNER. *(pointing to the back which is still hidden in clouds)* Heavy mists hang in the air. I'll liven these thin clouds with some lightning and thunder. I'll sweep the blue heavens clean.

(Donner mounts to an overhanging rock and swings his hammer. During what follows the mists gather around him.)

DONNER. Come down to me, mists. Donner is here, calling his hosts. As his hammer swings, sweep to his side.

(Donner disappears in the ever thickening and darkening cloud. Then his hammer stroke is heard to fall heavily on the rocks. A vivid flash of lightning breaks through the clouds, followed by a violent clap of thunder.)

DONNER. Brother, come here. Show what a bridge we can shape.

(Froh has also disappeared in the clouds. Suddenly the clouds separate. Donner and Froh are visible. A rainbow-bridge of dazzling radiance stretches from their feet over the valley to the castle, which gleams with utmost brilliance in the sunlight.)

FROH. This bridge to your home is light yet secure. You can cross it without danger.

Logi for once shows some emotion, amazement, "Your luck, Wotan, is un-be-liev-able. The chances against our gaining control in Nibelung were a thousand to one and we made it without a fumble. But *who* would have guessed its surrender to the teras would have started this. For more than two generations, ever since their manufacture was outlawed, those missiles have been aimed but not fired." He glances at FAFNER's and FASOLT's representatives who are adjusting and readjusting the television but getting no results. "Now, very likely, FASOLT is completely destroyed and FAFNER will be severely damaged. FAFNER struck first but I doubt if it will have many cities left in thirty minutes. Maybe not any."

Wotan says, "This luck, as you in your profound detachment call it, depresses me. It raises some questions that I must answer. I'd like to stay in Nibelung until the full story is learned and see the effect. Also that woman, Erda, haunts my thoughts. I'd like to see her again."

"Why linger here, Wotan?" Fricka asks. "By the terms of the treaty our own city can now be entered. And now it may be the greatest city in the world — the greatest by far. Imagine it. The world's greatest city is waiting to welcome its lord."

"I have compromised my ideals," Wotan says gloomily, "and that's a price too high for any city. Perhaps the dwarfs did not pay less for theirs. And the final bill has not yet been received. It could be that we have paid more."

Donner tells Wotan, "We should get out of here. Atomic fallout will be heavy and Nibelung will get it from all sides. There are some measures that can be taken to keep fallout at a minimum in Godsland. As soon as we're in the plane, I'll radio back and give the orders. Let's go now."

The sovereigns leave and just as they do FAFNER's and FASOLT's representatives get a new picture on television of an actual mushroom cloud, a siren is wailing, then comes a blinding flash, followed by total blackness.

The blackness is now everywhere.

In the full darkness the roar of planes is heard. There are sounds of explosives and flashes of light.

Then in total darkness the running lights of a plane are seen.

* * *

There is a switch to a radiant dawn with the sovereign's city in the left background. Wotan, Fricka, Donner, and Logi have just landed and are leaving their plane. The airport is the simple

WOTAN. *(absorbed in contemplation of the castle)* Look how the light of evening gilds all its turrets and towers with a glorious touch. In the light of morning, glittering proudly, it, standing masterless, beckoned to me. From morning to evening much toil and fear have gone into its winning. From the darkness of night it now offers us shelter. *(To Fricka)* So I greet my home. Let it heal my sorrow and fear. Come with me, wife. In Valhall safe we will live.

FRICKA. What is the meaning of the name "Valhall"? I never seem to have heard it.

WOTAN. That which, conquering fear, my fortitude brought triumphant to birth — let that explain the word.

(Wotan and Fricka go towards the bridge. Froh and Freia follow immediately, then Donner.)

LOGE. *(remaining in the foreground and looking after the gods)* They are hastening to their end, even while dreaming that they are strong and enduring. Almost ashamed am I to be of their number. A fancy allures me to wander forth as a flickering fire. Perhaps better to burn them than perish blind among the blind. Even if the gods were more godlike, that might be the better way. I need to consider. Who knows? *(He follows the gods as if unconcerned.)*

(From the valley, where they are invisible, the song of the Rhine-maidens is heard.)

THE THREE RHINE-MAIDENS. Rhinegold! Rhinegold! Rhinegold pure! How radiant and clear you once did shine on us. For your lost glory we are grieving. Give us our gold! Give us our gold! O give us our Rhinegold again!

WOTAN. *(about to set foot on the bridge, pauses and turns around.)* What mournful sounds do I hear?

backwoods sort, but various airport workers and sovereign guards are moving about. After an exchange of salutes, Donner asks the officer of the guard, "Are all arrangements in order for the entrance?"

The officer of the guard answers, "Everything is in order, Sir. The ground vehicle waiting there will take the Chief's party. The honor guard is standing by to pick you up on the other side of the bridge."

Wotan and the other sovereigns pause and stand silently contemplating the splendor of the city in the rising sun.

Wotan says quietly, "It glitters a little too much, like a machine-cut jewel set among dew drops. I hope its sparkling clearness comes from something more than simple contrast with a horrible night. Grief, fear and uncertainty have all gone into its construction; it's foundations may be shaky. But it shows no mark of its cost. Maybe it will be a new start to finer things." He turns to Fricka, "Let us go, Fricka, your desire is fulfilled. Enter with me now into Valhalla."

She asks as she takes his arm, "What meaning in your thoughts is suggested by Valhalla? In my experience that's a new word."

"An end result," he says, "which hopefully forgets the method that accomplished it — let that explain the word." They walk slowly toward the waiting vehicle. Donner falls in a pace behind.

Logi, who has remained in the foreground watching the sovereigns, muses aloud. "Are they really any different from the old establishment? Like all before them they are going toward their doom even while still dreaming that they are strong and enduring. Almost I'm ashamed to be of their number. With my knowledge of life, I can have no faith in their faith. Almost I think it would be better to sear them with my contempt and leave them, rather than go down as one blind among the blind." He makes a motion to go then hesitates in indecision. "Even if the gods were more godlike, I might be better free from my attachment so as to be amused and laugh whatever the outcome." Then, with a show of carelessness, he starts to follow the sovereigns.

The sound of singing comes from a television that is not visible but indicated by a watching and listening group of airport workers and warriors.

Wotan seems reluctant to continue on. He gives Fricka to Donner's arm, pauses, turns around, waits for Logi and calls to ask him, "What's that wailing sound I hear?"

111

LOGE. The Rhine-maidens are yearning for their lost glory.

WOTAN. Disturbing nixes! Quell their clamorous noise.

LOGE. *(calling down to the valley)* You in the water. Worry us no longer. Listen to Wotan's wish. You have seen the last of the Rhinegold. You can bask yourselves in the god's increased splendor.

(The gods laugh loudly and once more turn toward the bridge.)

THE THREE RHINE-MAIDENS. Rhinegold! Rhinegold! Rhinegold pure! Oh, if in the waves still shone our treasure pure. Only down in the waters can faith be found. Mean and false are all who revel above.

(As the gods slowly cross the bridge to the castle, the curtain falls.)

Logi explains, "Everyone is trying to get news of the world. They have managed to get a broadcast from Nibelung where no one seems to know what has really happened. So far they have only tuned in to some cabaret singers. Alber brought the three girls from the wilds in his heyday and their naivete at first made them very popular. I've met them. They are wiser now, and a little shopworn."

Wotan says, "Their song and their young pained voices coming out of Nibelung stirs too deeply for comfort something in my conscience." Wotan goes on alone and Logi falls behind again.

For a moment Logi watches those gathered about the television then calls toward them, "When all the world is considering only the fate of nations, what primordial spark within you, finds more important the sad songs of young maidens?"

No one hears him. No one answers. He answers himself. "Perhaps, after all, you are gods."

After watching them thoughtfully for a moment, he adds, "But your leader, who set free your mortal enemy, leads on unheedingly toward his doom — and yours."

He joins the sovereigns entering the waiting vehicles as the song continues:

"Wildgold! Wildgold! Wildgold pure! How radiant and pure we were when our life was yours. For your lost glory we are grieving. Give us our gold! Give us our gold! Oh, give us our wildgold again!"

"They are wiser now, and a little shopworn."

SOVEREIGN PRESS

Dedicated to Individual Sovereignty

We, of Sovereign Press, are intently aware that the opposing directions being taken by the two cultures need to be publicly defined and understood. Our aim is to assemble and make available sound, basic books that are brief and clear enough to provide a solid foundation under all active developments that seek to restore individual sovereignty — in the public arena or fully segregated.

Since Sovereign Press was established in 1968, our steady build-up of sales by reviews, by university instructors including our works in their courses, and by words passed from individual to individual has been gratifying evidence that perception continues to exist. We give booksellers the usual discounts and credit terms, and have widespread sales through wholesalers who buy for libraries, the academic community, and the few retail stores that still order special books for good customers. However, we are not geared to the usual mass promotion of "best sellers." Because most bookstores are now so geared, you cannot usually find our books in retail stores. To meet this condition we maintain full mail order facilities. Individual orders are welcome.

Publisher pays postage (including foreign) when payment
in U.S. funds is received with order

Take 40 percent discount on 10 or more copies same title.

SOVEREIGN PRESS, 326 Harris Rd., Rochester, WA 98579   USA

89278 LIFE'S MEANING. Marguerite Pedersen. Pedersen first attacks the dragons, themselves — the political and religious group-entities that destroy individual integrity. She then turns on the tightly woven weapon of word conditioning that group-entities use to keep individuals from being individuals. Finally she presents a completely new picture of natural relationships between living things, the universe, and the Primal Being that goes beyond all religions — including the "religion" of "materialism." This work will be a cherished find for all who have been turned off by the falseness of those who parrot glib explanations of life's meaning — or lack of meaning.
Permanent quality 5½ x 8½ paperback, 96 pages $5.00

79111 THE RING CYCLE. Melvin Gorham. This book contains in one volume Melvin Gorham's interpretation of Richard Wagner's THE VALKYRIE, SIEGFRIED, and GOTTERDAMMERUNG. Gorham sets this continuous story in the 21st century to permit the use of current references in translating the subconscious symbols into their present day counterparts. This adaptation to the 21st century setting makes an interesting background for Wagner's plot, which Gorham follows closely. In addition to supplying a clear interpretation of Wagner's incomparable work, the whole gives a cogent projection of the ultimate ideological, and physical, conflict to which current conditions are now leading.
79111   hardcover $9.00
79103   permanent quality 5½ x 8½ paperback, 144 pages $5.00

SOVEREIGN PRESS, 326 Harris Road, Rochester, WA   98579   U.S.A.

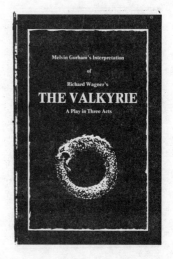

$4.00
paper
96 pages

**Melvin Gorham's Interpretation of Richard Wagner's
THE VALKYRIE, A Play in Three Acts.**

Review in **LIBRARY JOURNAL:**
Gorham's interpretation of *The Valkyrie* is set in the 21st Century. The warrior Hunding is portrayed as an official in the police state of Fafner, and the Valkyries are plane pilots who rescue wounded heroes from battle and take them to the gods' haven in Valhalla. Such adaptations to the 21st Century setting make an interesting background for Wagner's plot, which Gorham follows closely. Siegmund, the hero of the wildspeople, seeks the overthrow of the police state, and though Wotan, the leader of the "gods," wants Siegmund to win, he is bound by treaty not to help him. Thus when his daughter, the chief of the Valkyries, attempts to aid Siegmund, Wotan must exile her. The play has three male and 11 female parts, plus optional characters. Recommended for university theater departments or those seeking a play with potential for experimental staging.

- Susan F. Curtis, **LIBRARY JOURNAL**

Contains supplementary article, **THE MORALITY OF THE EARLY NORTHERN EUROPEANS,** by John Harland.

87243 paperback, 5 x 8, 96 pages $4.00

SOVEREIGN PRESS, 326 Harris Road, Rochester, WA   98579   U.S.A.

$5.00
paper
144 pages

84170 BRAVE NEW WORLD, A Different Projection. John Harland.

A rebel of the sixties generation has now matured and found words for his thoughts. In San Francisco John Harland, at nineteen, and an eighteen year old runaway named Jill, joined forces to create a new world.

Along with his examination of various lifestyles he and Jill explored, he examines what's wrong with the establishment, with emphasis on manipulation by word-conditioning, and looks at many well-known doomsday books, such as Huxley's *Brave New World,* Orwell's *Nineteen Eighty-four,* and Zamyatin's *We.* Harland may not be voicing the consensus thoughts of the sixties rebels but his world is startlingly new — and exclusively for the brave. Suitable for classroom discussion.

Permanent quality 5½ × 8½ paperback 144 pages $5.00

Excerpt from a review of **BRAVE NEW WORLD, A Different Projection** by John Harland:

"As I predicted, the brighter lights of the rebellion of the sixties would only show their color after the hubbub subsided."

— Burton Frye, REGIONAL NEWS, Lake Geneva, Wis.

BRAVE NEW WORLD, A Different Projection by John Harland recommended for library purchase by BOOKLIST. See full review in BOOKLIST 9-15-78.

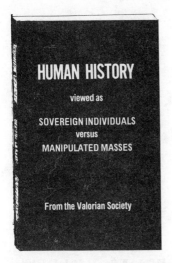

86235 HUMAN HISTORY, viewed as SOVEREIGN INDIVIDUALS versus MANIPULATED MASSES, Valorian Society. This joint work by a secluded group of highly perceptive writers views the historical and current problem of humans as two opposing cultures that cannot be mixed. The culture of sovereign individuals has had to fight a two front battle against manipulated masses — manipulated by overt force in the East, and manipulated by brainwashing in the Western World. TV brainwashing by internationalists and the unconstitutional use of money as manipulative force in the U.S. now threatens to produce one worldwide totalitarian human entity.

5 x 8, 112 pages, paperback $4.00

84197 CAMP 38. Jill von Konen.

This is the Jill of John Harland's *Brave New World.* Her narrative presentation covers all aspects of day-to-day life in a fully developed "Brave New World" as projected by those who form secluded Valorian Society groups. It bears the subtitle: *Current model of NORTHERN EUROPEAN LIFESTYLE before Christianity.* This was added because Jill's projection of their current individual sovereignty lifestyle revealed that it will *necessarily* follow the same pattern as that which originally produced the people of Northern European heritage.

Permanent quality 5½ × 8½ paperback 208 pages $6.00

SOVEREIGN PRESS, 326 Harris Road, Rochester, WA   98579   U.S.A.

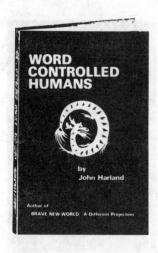

$5.00

paper

128 pages

81138 WORD CONTROLLED HUMANS, A Brief History.
John Harland. Brief and crystal clear, this would be an
admirable basic work before any other history is studied in
the schools. The two major conflicting concepts of how life
should be lived are described as cultural directions that came
into conflict before that conflict reached a climax in the
teachings and crucifixion of Jesus. The Holy Roman Church's
use of a *false* Christianity to promote a theocracy is sharply
portrayed as the destroyer of both the teachings of Jesus and
the Northern European cultural direction.

Then the American attempt to regain our cultural heritage
of individual integrity is examined. The two hundred year
long losing battle is covered from the perspective of religion,
government, and money. Expanding to the worldwide scene,
Harland looks at the errors made by the Germans under
Hitler in trying to recover from the destructive effects of
theocracy. He keeps his eye on what is significant rather than
merely sensational.

This brief history puts the problems of the human species
into a context where effective action to correct them can be
seen as a present possibility.

81138	Hardcover	$9.00
8112X	5¼x8¼ permanent quality paperback	$5.00

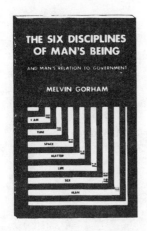

87251 THE CRUISE OF THE SKULD, by Marguerite Pedersen. A captive yacht, a kidnapped crew and passengers, and a modern day "Flying Dutchman" form the background for this unusual novel. Ten highly intelligent young individualists — ready, willing, and able to give the best possible direction to their lives — intersperse action with penetrating arguments about the current human condition, and the possibilities of correcting it. This is a thought stimulating examination of the basic causes underlying our present individual-destroying "civilization."
Paperback, 5 x 8, 160 pages $5.00

83162 THE SIX DISCIPLINES OF MAN'S BEING, Melvin Gorham. Gorham is a profound philosopher who follows no established school of philosophy. This work presents a concept of time, space, and matter that is highly controversial — and highly cogent. It follows the accepted viewpoint of organic evolution, but sheds new light on the meaning of life by comparing the direction pointed by evolutionary development with inherited memory. The whole posits a radically new "ultimate frame of reference" for total reality.
5 x 8, 128 pages, paperback $5.00

Excerpt from a review of **THE SIX DISCIPLINES OF MAN'S BEING and MAN'S RELATION TO GOVERNMENT**
"Melvin Gorham will be read and studied for centuries after today's bestseller authors have been buried with the people who found their books amusing."

— Burton Frye, RFD News, Belleview, Ohio

SOVEREIGN PRESS, 326 Harris Road, Rochester, WA   98579   U.S.A.

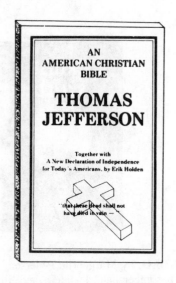

AN
AMERICAN CHRISTIAN
BIBLE

**THOMAS
JEFFERSON**

Together with
A New Declaration of Independence
for Today's Americans. by Erik Holden

"that these dead shall not
have died in vain —

$5.00
paper
128 pages

82146 AMERICAN CHRISTIAN BIBLE, extracted by Thomas Jefferson. Jefferson's extracts from the Bible were not made public until 1902 and are still suppressed. The reason for this is important to every American, and especially to those of Northern European heritage.

The God called "Father" by Jesus was a God of individuals; this made the teachings of Jesus fully compatible with the aboriginal religion of the Northern Europeans. History has been distorted to cover up this fact. The religion of the Jews, who violently condemned Jesus for blaspheming against their *groupism* religion, was imposed upon, identified with, and used to mutilate the teachings of Jesus.

Thomas Jefferson, who carefully worded reference to a creator in the Declaration of Independence "Nature and Nature's God," considered himself a *real* Christian — but felt that he had to keep private his own version of the Bible; he had used scissors to cut away from the words and story of Jesus the mutilating Judaic injections.

This book contains a reproduced photocopy of Jefferson's work, along with an up-to-the-minute examination by Erik Holden of Christianity, biological development, and the all important relationship between religion, state, and individual sovereignty.
Permanent quality 8¼ x 5¼ paperback $5.00

$5.00

paper

128 pages

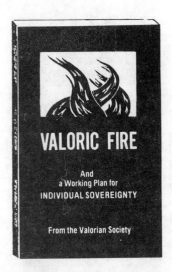

84189 VALORIC FIRE and a WORKING PLAN FOR INDI-VIDUAL SOVEREIGNTY. From the Valorian Society.

This unusual book first sets forth an imaginary campfire conference of people with varied pasts who are seeking to form a totally new human relationship based on a new morality. As brands. from the burning, they readily reject the theocratic pseudo-morality that has already scorched the earth. Approaching every possible discussion with an alerted suspicion of groupism, they probe for some *new* morality that may be manifest by Nature.

A second section clearly states Nature's morality, dismisses *all* laws imposed on individuals by groups as immoral, and proposes agreements between individuals to limit group power. The proposed "new" agreements are found to be the *old* ones that governed the people of Northern Europe before Christianity. This work gives the precise wording of the seven points of agreement that play a big part in John Harland's *Brave New World,* and in Jill von Konen's *Camp 38.* Also it describes how they may be adapted to form functioning agreements for a current survival group, or for a current group wanting a better way of life than the world of maniupulated zombis.

Permanent quality 5½ × 8½ paperback 128 pages $5.00

SOVEREIGN PRESS, 326 Harris Road, Rochester, WA   98579   U.S.A.

83154 THE FORCE UNDERLYING MASS WARFARE. This is the strategy of the Individual Sovereignty Society for dealing with the causes behind the atomic bomb and all mass warfare—and for restoring constitutional Government in the United States. Emphasis is on the unconstitutional power to control the value of U.S. money given to the Federal Reserve Bank, and the unconstitutional power of censorship given to those controlling radio and television broadcast stations. Contains information about objectives, organization, and qualifications for membership in the ISS.

24 page brochure $1.00

84200 HUMAN CULTURE OF HUMANS, by the Valorian Society. This work focuses on the problem created by the media-pushed breeding for mass manipulation as it now exists in the United States — and on the historical background of the problem. The current catalog of Sovereign Press, *An Evaluation of Our American Heritage,* is extracted from this fuller work.

32 page brochure $1.00

8826X AN EVALUATION OF OUR AMERICAN HERITAGE. A statement of publishing policy and a catalog of Sovereign Press Books.

32 page brochure $1.00

SOVEREIGN PRESS, 326 Harris Rd., Rochester, WA 98579   USA

ORDER FORM

To: **SOVEREIGN PRESS, 326 Harris Rd., Rochester, WA 98579 U.S.A.**

Publisher pays postage (including foreign) when payment in U. S. funds is enclosed with order. Take 40% discount 10 or more copies same title.

Quantity			Extension
	American Christian Bible	5.00	
	Brave New World	5.00	
	Camp 38	6.00	
	Cruise of the Skuld	5.00	
	Force Under. Mass Warfare	1.00	
	Human Culture of Humans	1.00	
	Human History	4.00	
	Life's Meaning	5.00	
	Our American Heritage	1.00	
	The Rhinegold	5.00	
	Ring Cycle, paper	5.00	
	Ring Cycle, hardcover	9.00	
	Six Disciplines	5.00	
	The Valkyrie	4.00	
	Valoric Fire	5.00	
	Word Controlled Humans,pap.	5.00	
	Word Controlled Humans,hc.	9.00	
Sales Tax (Washington Residents)			
Total (enclosed)			

Name _____

Address _____

_____ zip _____

127